Guarded by Dragons

Praise for *Tolkien's Gown*

'This is essential reading for any booklover, but it is also a supreme example of a natural and skilled storyteller at work. It is wonderfully paced and full of rich and fascinating detail' Colm Tóibín

'Dealer Rick Gekoski's account of some of the rare books that have passed through his hands is packed with tantalising trivia, laced with great humour and full of detailed descriptions that will have any bibliophile slavering' *Independent on Sunday*

'Hugely entertaining account of the great books and their worth as literature – and as first editions – by the fabulously infectious American bibliophile. Think Bill Bryson, only on books' *Tatler*

'Rick Gekoski's *Tolkien's Gown* is an irresistible mix of droll humour, shrewd literary criticism and fascinating anecdote, by a dealer in the fetishistic world of modern first editions. The perfect bedside book for bibliophiles' David Lodge, *Sunday Telegraph*

'Page after page of delight ... a worthy enough counterpart to the essays of Charles Lamb' *Sunday Times*

'Rick Gekoski, a modern-first dealer who has dragged many a huge beast of a book back from the jungle and brought it blinking in the spotlight like a 40ft ape ... Gekoski likes to be around a better class of book than the rest of us (Ted Hughes' copy of Sylvia Plath's *Colossus*; *Sons and Lovers* in transcendentally rare dustwrapper); and by skill, luck and chutzpah has managed to' *Guardian*

Guarded by Dragons

Encounters with Rare Books and Rare People

RICK GEKOSKI

CONSTABLE

CONSTABLE

First published in Great Britain in 2021 by Constable

1 3 5 7 9 10 8 6 4 2

Copyright © Rick Gekoski, 2021

The moral right of the author has been asserted.

A CIP catalogue record for this book
is available from the British Library.

ISBN: 978-1-47213-385-4 (hardback)
ISBN: 978-1-40871-541-3 (trade paperback)

Typeset in Bembo by Hewer Text UK Ltd, Edinburgh
Printed and bound in Great Britain by Clays Ltd, Elcograf S.p.A.

Papers used by Constable are from well-managed
forests and other responsible sources.

Constable
An imprint of
Little, Brown Book Group
Carmelite House
50 Victoria Embankment
London EC4Y 0DZ

An Hachette UK Company
www.hachette.co.uk

www.littlebrown.co.uk

For Peter Selley and Peter Straus

Contents

'Every treasure is guarded by dragons.
That's how you can tell it's valuable.'

Saul Bellow, *Herzog*

Foreword

I have been buying and selling rare books and manuscripts for over fifty years, and am now of an age when most people have long retired, and at which booksellers write their memoirs. When I began making my first tentative purchases of first editions, in the middle 1960s, the English rare book trade was stuffy, hidebound and unsophisticated. Catalogues were cyclo-styled on to cheap paper. Orders could be made by post, tele-gram, or even telephone. Customers, largely male, thought of themselves as gentlemen, and occasionally were. Librarians bought books avidly.

It was a very long time ago, longer than the number fifty suggests. In May of 1966, *The Times*, in a brilliant bit of journal-istic innovation, decided to put news on its front page. Homosexuality and abortion were still illegal. The Pill came, jumbo jets went. Children were still children. Adults wrote things with pens, on paper.

In comparison, the changes in the rare book world, while obvious, were modest. Trade has widened, democratised, and become newsworthy. Courses, both academic and extramural, have sprouted internationally, with attendant symposia and conferences. Many students who go to such rare book seminars may think of themselves as receiving a training to become a dealer. They are not, it's the wrong place and the wrong goal. There are only two things a rare book dealer must know: at what price is a book buyable and at what higher price one might sell it. You learn that best by working in a bookshop, a good one, handling and cataloguing and thinking about thousands of books over many years: serving an apprenticeship before starting on your own. You will find such a background in most of the leading dealers. I don't have it myself, and many of my failings as a bookseller come from this lack of an immersive background: I entered the rare book world as an academic and a collector, with some knowledge and taste, but without the necessary experience.

In those days, the rare book world was cloistered, like some kind of private club. Nowadays, regular and surprisingly popular slots on television and radio are given over to the subject of rare books, the discoveries and occasional villainies. Contemporary catalogues of even mid-market booksellers are finely printed in colour on good-quality paper, as if issued by an upscale department store. They look expensive, sometimes even *chic*. I have mixed feelings about this slickness, but my instincts, like those of Groucho Marx, are against it. It feels less authentic, a world apart from its subject, crassly assimilated to unbookish paradigms of marketing and branding. The increasing importance of the condition of a rare book, whether it has a dust wrapper in unblemished state, is surely a sign of this inappropriate commodification.

I shouldn't be so sniffy, for I had a role in this modernising trend, when in 1982 I issued my first catalogue, which included pictures of many of the items, and had a textual levity, which I liked to think of as wit, which rather shocked the established members of the trade. Since that time, I have occasionally been asked to speak on topics relating to the rare book world, and written about the subject quite a bit.

A moderator at a conference recently asked me what lessons I had learnt, and what advice – he called it 'wisdom' – I might impart to young collectors and dealers.

'None,' I said.

'Can you explain?'

'How do you define a horse?' I responded.

He looked puzzled.

The reference was to *Hard Times*, in which the strictly utilitarian schoolmaster, Mr Gradgrind, who cares only about facts, seeks a definition of a horse. First he asks Girl Number 20, Sissy Jupe, who (though her father works at the circus) is dumbfounded and tongue-tied. The question is then offered to the teacher's pet, Bitzer, who gives the required definition: 'Quadruped. Graminivorous. Forty teeth, namely twenty-four grinders, four eye-teeth, and twelve incisive. Sheds coat in the spring; in marshy countries, sheds hoofs, too. Hoofs hard, but requiring to be shod ... Age known by marks in mouth.'

Edit this cunningly and you might almost apply the definition to book dealers.

Sissy Jupe knows what a horse is: her (ostensive) definition would involve a walk to a paddock and a lot of pointing, after which her interlocutor would be able to point one out, too. Bitzer's definition is generic, and it is hard to imagine who might find it helpful, for it fails to generate a memorable image.

Which is exactly how I feel about most courses, symposia and conferences about the rare book trade. I like to think of myself as its Sissy Jupe, and am as thoroughly convinced as the next girl that, if you want to learn about something, you need to know how and where to point, to be particular and specific. Don't ask me to generalise and to produce formulae. I could but I won't, it's boring and done half-to-death elsewhere. It is the job of the young to learn things, and of the old to forget them.

In the words of William Blake: 'To generalise is to be an idiot.' I've read and listened to many biblio-idiots (and been one myself) and the irony is that most of them/us are extremely interesting, not from a lecturer's podium, but sitting round a dinner table after a few drinks, telling stories.

Many of the major topics, themes, and books on my subject only come to life when they light upon particular deals, books, and episodes. On what the late Texas dealer John Jenkins called 'capers', a nicely chosen word with a suggestion of dangerous naughtiness. By way of contrast, most works for and by bibliophiles are, well, unexciting: I skim such tomes like the teenagers of my generation used to flip through the pages of novels, looking for the sexy bits.

The following chapters are an attempt to avoid answering the question 'What have you learnt?' by substituting the more pertinent 'What have you experienced?' Because, when the moderators have turned off their microphones, the audience closed their notebooks, and sessions of the conference end, we participants repair to bar and table where the real fun begins, tales of commerce, frustrated or rewarded, that amuse, tease and stick in the memory. Such stories run to type, being based on the archetype of the treasure hunt: as Saul Bellow so wryly observed, there's something enticing and valuable out there, the intrepid hunter-dealer seeks it out, but it is guarded by a jealous owner-dragon, and other hunters are circling.

The treasure being pursued is often the accumulation of a lifetime, and though the reasons for disposing of it may be pressing, they are often painful. That is why dragons sit at the front of their caves, their gleaming goodies behind them. In my experience, some are fiercer than others, but all require careful handling, and I do not possess what UA Fanthorpe calls 'diplomas in dragon management'. I get on well with some, others leave scorch marks. All leave stories.

For me – you may say, alas, I sometimes do, too – writing non-fiction is always a form of memoir, and my own role in the history and future of literary treasures I have handled is my recurrent subject. And, no, I will not begin with some definition of 'treasure', which would miss the point and spoil the fun. In the following chapters I will try to give each object its just placement in the literary context that it inhabits, but these descriptions are narrated as part of an adventure in the world of important objects: seeking the most exciting things, encountering unusual people and unforeseen dangers.

So, as dear Sissy Jupe knew what to point to, may I offer the following stories, which are roughly chronological, starting at almost the beginning and ending at not quite the end. Though they occasionally overlap, they can be read independently. I hope they will entertain, and if you feel you might also learn from them, well . . . that's up to you.

Rick Gekoski, April 2021

1

On Sabbatical with DH Lawrence

First class! At the Pan Am check-in desk, we were greeted deferentially, directed to a fancy lounge, and soon boarded the flight to New York, well ahead of the econo-masses. A stewardess escorted us up the aisle to the front bulkhead, plumped up everything, seated Barbara, and helped put baby Anna in a hanging bassinette in front of us. Both of them beamed. As I sat down, the woman across the aisle leant across, had a good look at Anna, and said some appropriate goo-goo things, before leaning back in her seat awaiting her glass of champagne.

I settled down happily in my unaccustomed comfort zone, the upgrade a treat from my father as our little family flew to New York, where I would be spending the next months. Following my postgraduate years at Oxford, I'd been appointed to a Lectureship in English at the University of Warwick in 1971. The first, heady years of teaching were absorbing, as I read and thought and articulated with a passion that rather surprised me, and I soon found that I was already eligible for sabbatical leave. This was a matter of statutory entitlement rather than merit, for I was already manifesting that scholarly mediocrity that was to characterise my academic career. I love talking and listening, the give and take of the seminar and tutorial system, but have neither the taste nor the ability to do sustained academic research.

I'd finished my Oxford DPhil on Joseph Conrad, and wangled a contract with Methuen for a critical book on DH Lawrence, on which I was making scant progress. It bored me. Embarking on the research for this volume, I began to collect first editions of Lawrence, which was of much greater interest, igniting a passion that was to last for the next decade.

The sabbatical couldn't have come at a better, or a worse, time, as my mother was dying of cancer at her home on Long Island. So when I was granted leave for the first term of 1975, we could get to her bedside while she still had a few weeks to live. I was dreading it: we were already exhausted by new parenthood, and my mother's imminent death was certain to be harrowing. She was only fifty-six, and had still not recovered from her divorce five years earlier. 'I got a royal screwing!' she would announce, insisting that my sister and I adopt the same description of her plight. In good health she'd been an angry woman, in her decline she was furious and inconsolable.

On the plane, after we finished our glasses of champagne and prepared to take off, Barbara leant across to me.

'Do you know who that is?' she whispered.

'No idea. Somebody?'

'Petula Clark!' she said. 'Isn't she lovely?'

Anna and Petula slept for most of the flight, while Barbara and I enjoyed ourselves, drinking and watching films. When my father met us at JFK we were profuse in our thanks, and he offered his usual benign smile, as we carried the luggage to the car, ready for the hour-long drive to Huntington, on the north shore of Long Island. He dropped us in front of my mother's house, but did not come in, which he would have been required to do on bended knee. Entering the house – she could still get out of bed for a few hours – we exchanged sad perfunctory embraces, and soon began to set ourselves up in a small, economy-class bedroom that was hardly comfortable for an exhausted young family. Over the following weeks my mother was retracted, clenched and unreconciled to God or her children. She died on 8 December 1974.

We left her house a few weeks later, and found an apartment in Park Slope, in Brooklyn. It was a thoroughly miserable time. In the early mornings, I would take our sleepless, grizzly baby off to the local deli for breakfast. This gave her mother a chance for some desperately needed sleep, and me a recurring opportunity to eat lox and eggs, and pickles from the overflowing free pickles bowl. Anna would drink her bottle of milk, and renew her grizzling. Teething, colic, lack of sleep? Any or all of the above, and more. One morning, anxious to shut her mouth, I stuck a pickle in it.

She looked bemused. Put her little hands up to take it by both sides as if it were a bottle of milk, sucked on it, and made a pucker face.

'That'll stop your *kvetching*!' I said, reaching to take it out.

She wouldn't let go, as a look of bliss crossed her features, unseen since she'd lost contact with her mother's breasts a few months previously. For the rest of our stay in Brooklyn, she and I would be waiting in front of the deli when it opened at

7.00am, and made our way to our regular booth in the window. The elderly waitress, after a bit of tut-tutting, would bring me coffee, lox and eggs, and insert Anna's pickle. A group of little old Jewish ladies were rapt, torn between amazement, disapproval, and delight at the unusual baby.

'Look at him, already with the pickles!' At first I thought they were referring to me, but they had universally decided that Anna was a boy, with that noble brow and receding hairline, puffy red cheeks, and indomitable will, which may have reminded them of the greatest of all Englishmen.

'Aw!' said the waitress on our first meeting, peering down intently at the baby. I could sense her rejecting the usual possibilities: 'cutie', 'darling', 'sweetie pie' ... no chucking under the chin for this one.

'What's his name?' she asked.

'Winston,' I said.

A proud father, I soon noticed that he/she had become something of a local celebrity, the tables next to ours filled quickly, and a small group would gather at the window to watch us. Anna played the crowd, and would sometimes take the pickle in her right hand, and wave it. The crowd was enchanted, and waved right back. Anna would grin at the discovery of this new power, as if a conductor with her orchestra. She then added to her sucking repertoire a determined gumming, which slowly reduced the top, then the middle of the pickle to mush. I'd put her yellow plastic bib on and it accumulated bits of slimy green goo. When the time came to leave, she refused to relinquish her treat, and gnawed at it in her pushchair as we made our way to the park, and I lit my first cigar of the day.

It's a long way, is it, from a pickle-eating baby to first editions of DH Lawrence? Not at all, it was a five-minute walk. I had discovered through the *Yellow Pages* that just down the road was a second-hand bookseller named William Hauser, whose substantial stock was displayed on the ground floor of a brownstone.

I felt guilty, leaving Barbara with a de-pickled, discontented baby for most of the day, but of course, I was going out to read and do research on my book on DHL. That's what sabbaticals are for. Instead of going directly to the library, though, I would stop at Bill Hauser's to go through his surprisingly large offering of Lawrence first editions. Scholars need first editions, don't they? It's better to work from the original text than from some later iteration! I had my rationale ready to mouth in case Barbara ever found out my secret, but how could she? Unless, of course, I came home clutching my treasures. Best have the dealer post them back to the University to await my return.

I've just used the term 'treasures' loosely, and abashedly. There was nothing particularly rare on Bill Hauser's shelves, though in those days it could be surprisingly difficult to locate even a common book. What made his Lawrences so enticing was not that they were rare, but that they were cheap. Not treasures, then, better than treasures: bargains! Bill was nearing retirement, and anxious to sell off his inventory, and he'd taken a shine to my naïve recurrent enthusiasm. Having compiled a handwritten list of his stock, I would buy a couple of books, cross them off, and think obsessively about which others I might be able to afford. I went back five times. His low prices got lower and lower.

Over the course of those weeks, Anna consumed pickles as regularly and with as much delight as I consumed Lawrences. More! More! Her habit was both more unusual and cheaper than mine; pickles at a Jewish deli are the ultimate bargain, though you cannot make a profit from them unless you're a pickle dealer. But you can make a significant loss. I discovered this only a couple of years later, when my sister Ruthie gave birth to her first child, Matthew. During one of my visits to her on Long Island, observing that the baby was a bit fretful, and by now much the same age as Anna had been when I introduced her to her (life-long) habit and delight, I approached Matthew's pushchair and popped a pickle in his mouth. He sucked on it, much as Anna had.

Two minutes later, he was crying and had abandoned his pickle; five minutes later, his face turned red; ten minutes later it had swollen to twice its size. Twenty minutes later, he was in the Emergency Room at Huntington Hospital.

Ruthie explained to the doctor what had happened.

'A pickle! What sort of idiot would feed a pickle to a six-month-old baby?'

Ruthie pointed me out, standing somewhat to the side.

'That one!'

'Babies like pickles . . .' I began.

In the course of my visits to Bill Hauser, I bought first editions of the Lawrence novels *The White Peacock*, *Sons and Lovers*, *The Rainbow*, *Women in Love*, *The Lost Girl*, and *Kangaroo*; and of his other books: *Love among the Haystacks*, *The Widowing of Mrs Holroyd*, *Assorted Articles*, *Amores*, *Psychoanalysis and the Unconscious*, and *Maestro Don Gesualdo*. But with the delight of acquiring the books came an unexpected conundrum. The books were so cheap (I paid the equivalent of £41 for the lot) that they could clearly be sold in the UK at a profit. Were they keepers, or sellers? Was I a collector, or a dealer, or some sort of can't-make-up-his-mind hybrid? Over the next few years I sold most of them, for a total of £333. A dealer then? But I spent the profits on more Lawrences, in better condition. A collector?

In 1975, books were cheap, but also hard to find, which was why the Hauser DHLs were such a treat. Those days, when one called a book 'rare', it was indeed rare, unlike today when even most desirable and scarcest first editions are common, though still expensive. I couldn't even purchase – I tried for years – a copy of the standard *Bibliography of DH Lawrence*, by Warren Roberts. Eventually I gave up, photocopied the example in our University Library, and had it bound up with some extra blank pages on which to record the history of my Lawrence acquisitions and sales.

In general, I am not a note-taker, nor am I in the least well organised. I cannot fill a filing cabinet with carefully sorted papers, am incapable of sustained research, lose and fail to pay bills, do not pay my taxes on time unless someone does it with – by which I mean for – me. So when I recently returned to my handmade copy of Roberts, I was astounded by the meticulous efficiency of my 1970s annotations. Thus I know which books I bought from Bill Hauser, and to whom I sold them, and how I used that money to replace them with copies in better condition, which I then sold. Collectors call this compulsive desire to find an even better copy, 'upgrading'.

By way of example? *Sons and Lovers*. I bought my first copy for $10 from Hauser in 1975, sold it in 1978 to Blackwell's in Oxford for £42, and soon bought a better copy from London's William Forster for £75. Which I then sold for £100 the next year, because in 1979 I bought the ultimate copy, from Blackwell's. It was from the library of Dennis Wheatley, a fine copy in a dust wrapper missing two small pieces from the front cover, but otherwise clean and white. It was the only copy they, or I, had ever seen on the market, and it still is. I was lucky enough to pop into Blackwell's the very day they were sending the catalogue out, and I snapped it up – think turtle, and jaws – for £350.

Unlike work on the putative critical book, which was glacially slow and unenthusiastic over these years, my collecting was focused, passionate and highly organised. I entered handwritten lists in my handmade copy of Roberts, not only of every DHL book I had owned and disowned, but all those sold at auction and at all major dealers. I probably knew more about DHL prices than, well, anybody. It was manic, obsessional, and out of character.

By the start of the 1980s, I had a pretty good DHL collection, for someone of my limited means, but had made scant headway on my book on Lawrence, which, though promised for early arrival at the publishers, never got beyond Chapter 3. My line of thought, to give it a grand name, was that Lawrence had a radical new epistemology, in which 'knowledge' is garnered not through the mind, but through the viscera: the heart, the stomach and, particularly, if rather oddly, the bowels. I gave a seminar paper on this topic to my fellow members of the English Department, who found it an uncongenial description of how they knew things.

I was still young enough, just, to regard myself as promising. But looked at with a strict eye, this only meant that I kept making promises, and then breaking them. Within a couple of years, I had reneged on the contract for the Lawrence book without putting anything substantial in its place. This effort at an academic treatise having fallen flat, I contemplated instead – a better idea! – writing a novel about an academic who is trying to write a book about Lawrence, and whose situation and marriage mirror those of Lawrence and Frieda. This was a genuinely promising idea, but I never managed to write more than a few pages. In 1997 Geoff Dyer wrote a book on a very similar theme – *Out of Sheer Rage* – much better than I could have.

In those days, you had a personal bank manager. Mine was called Robin, and he worked from a modest cubbyhole at Lloyds in Leamington Spa. If I wanted to talk with him, I could make an appointment, which was rather formal, or might just pop in on the off-chance to have a chat. It was soon clear to Robin that I was incapable of living within my means. Robin would occasionally point this out to me a trifle disapprovingly, but unthreateningly. Might it be possible, he asked mildly, for me to curb my spending?

No, I stood firm. 'Listen, Robin, at the overdraft interest rates you're charging, you ought to hold a party every time I come in ...'

'You know,' he said in measured tones as if speaking to a child or a naïve colonial visitor, 'we don't think like that in England.'

'I know,' I said shaking my head sadly, 'it's no wonder the country is such a mess.'

There was a pregnant pause. 'What can I do for you?'

'I want to borrow a thousand pounds. You know . . . on my overdraft?'

Can pauses get pregnanter?

'Ah . . . yes. A thousand pounds . . . Indeed. Do tell me why you need it, because . . .'

'I want to buy a collection of DH Lawrence first editions . . .'

I wish he'd said something, but he just slurped some water and slumped into his chair.

'. . . And I need it in cash.'

'In cash?'

'Yes, cash. And I need it in the next two days. I have to act fast!'

The previous day I'd received rather an odd phone call, from someone called Anthony (or perhaps it was Antonio) who described himself as an 'antique dealer from Wales'. He'd had my name from a mutual acquaintance who dealt in second-hand books, and lived in North Wales.

'I'm told you like the DH Lawrence books?' he said. He had some sort of accent, not Welsh. Hard to place.

'I do. What do you have?'

'I just bought a big collection of his first editions from an old lady . . .'

Ah, the proverbial little old lady. Not a good sign.

'What's in it? Do you have a list?'

'I'll read it to you,' he said.

I grabbed a notepad and pencil from my bedside table drawer. There was a substantial run of rarities: two of the signed first editions of Lady Chatterley, the scarcest signed issues of the poetry books, and most of the major novels. All, I was assured, 'look real nice!' Altogether there were twenty-odd books, many of which I did not have in my own collection, others of which might be sold at a profit if they were as good as he claimed. Perfect for me, both dealer and collector: buy books, keep some, sell some, buy more books.

'I'm interested,' I said, 'but of course I'd need to see them. How much do you want?'

'They're only for sale as a collection. No cherry-picking. And the price it is not negotiable. A thousand pounds ...'

'Sounds a bit tight, but I'd like a look at them ...' I began.

'... in cash!' he said.

'Well, that might take a little arranging,' I replied, having minus £218 in my bank account, 'but I might be able to swing it. What's your phone number? I'll get back to you.'

'I'll call you,' he said, and hung up.

I immediately rang my friend in North Wales to check out this so-called antique dealer, but his phone number had been cut off. This was not uncommon with Welsh second-hand book dealers in those days, but it added to my growing unease.

In the time it's taken me to recount this bit of back story, Robin was thoughtfully ruminating on my request for an extended overdraft. In cash.

'One question ...' he said.

'Of course.'

'How do you know these books are worth a thousand pounds?'

I leant genially over his desk. 'I wouldn't buy them otherwise, would I? I'll need to resell the best ones in order to pay you back.'

Twenty minutes later I exited Lloyds Bank, an envelope with twenty £50 notes tucked securely in my pocket, with my hand over it. I walked home carefully, looking both right and left as I made my way amongst the not necessarily innocent Leamingtonians.

A few days later the phone rang ... too early in the morning.

'Issat Rick?' The accent sounded Italian.

'Yes. Who's that?'

'Is Tony. You know, about the books.'

I know a lot of Tonys and a lot of books. It was 8.00am for Christ's sake.

'Books?'

'Books! You know! DH Lawrence!'

Ah, those books. 'Right.'

'You got the cash?'

'I have.'

'OK, meet me under the big clock in the concourse at Birmingham New Street Station. Friday at 12.00.'

He didn't ask if it was convenient. He knew I was keen, and may well have known that university lecturers have a lot of free time. To do research and to write books.

'How will I recognise you?'

'I'll recognise you,' he said.

'But ...' He'd hung up. Are antique dealers always so peremptory? If he was one. But if he wasn't, what was he? And what was he up to?

Lying beside me, Barbara had listened to the call. She'd been sceptical about this transaction from the beginning. Though she realised that book collectors and dealers are mad, she said this little caper 'smelt fishy'.

'I agree,' I said. 'But what can I do? It's a really good opportunity ...'

'Too good! And there's you off to meet a stranger with a thousand quid in your pocket!'

'Yeah, but it's in a railway station! What's he going to do ... gun me down?'

She thought about this for a moment and admitted it was unlikely.

'If I were you,' she said, 'I'd take someone with me ... if I were you.'

'You mean, like a bodyguard?'

'I mean like Malcolm.'

When I joined the English Faculty at Warwick in January of 1971, Malcolm was a first-year student in my Introduction to Modern Literature seminar. It was clear after only a few hours in his company that he had read as much as I, thought about it at least as carefully, and was a man of strong and considered opinion. One of the pleasures of my first year's teaching was that my students were not all that much younger than me, and many of them became lifelong friends. Like me, Malcolm was twenty-six. Given that he was gregarious, extremely articulate and mad on sports, we fell right into each other's friend-catchment-areas. He became a close friend in his Warwick time, and we kept in touch for many years afterwards.

None of these qualities, of course, would recommend him as a bodyguard. Nor was he physically prepossessing, but he was feisty, did not take any bullshit, and had a nose for an emerging problem. Fiercely loyal, Malcolm was a good man to have at your side, whatever the argument, unless you were having one with him. That happened, too, and was usually fun.

As we played snooker together one afternoon, I explained my situation, and need of his services.

He lined up his shot, missed – we both did a lot of that – and leant on his cue.

'I don't understand. Why do you need me to buy some books?'

'Don't you see? It's some sort of set-up. Why this anonymous meeting? Why the insistence on cash?'

'Seems OK to me. Dealers are like that, avoiding tax and all ...'

'Ah, but Malcolm, there's one thing I haven't told you yet!'

'What's that?'

'I think he's Italian.'

Being a (near) New Yorker, I knew a certain cross-section of Italians exactly for what they are, and what money laundering is. And they're smart guys, the Mob, you can only live off extortion, drugs and prostitution for so long. You need to branch out.

Malcolm looked puzzled.

'What he's going to do, attack you with a pizza?'

By the time we finished the game, he had agreed to come, on the promise of a good lunch and a couple of beers. Though he had the grace not to say it, he had immediately diagnosed that I was more likely to experience a breakdown than a shakedown, and might well be in need of psychological, rather than pugilistic, support.

On Friday we arrived at New Street Railway Station a few minutes before 12.00pm, and walked round casing the joint.

'What are we looking for?' asked Malcolm. 'A fleet of 1939 Packards with men in black suits and machine guns?'

'Very funny,' I said, keeping my eyes peeled for suspicious characters. It was a railway station. In Birmingham. Almost everyone was a suspicious character. Especially me.

At 11.59am, we stationed ourselves exactly beneath the giant clock on the wall 30ft above us. A minute later we were approached by a middle-aged man with a red face that had taken its fair share of drink, a dirty white shirt, blue tie at half mast, and a tweed suit by way of disguise.

He looked at me closely.

'Rick, right?'

I allowed that I was, indeed.

'I'm Tony.' He offered a hand for shaking, which didn't seem to have any weapon in it more dangerous than a small cigar, which he shifted to the left.

'And this is my friend Malcolm, he's an expert on DH Lawrence ...'

Tony shook his hand, too. We were getting on well, so far.

'Follow me,' said Tony, making his way towards the main exit. 'I've parked right outside, but it's a no-waiting zone, so we'll have to move the car.' We were approaching a shabby dark-green Volvo estate, of the sort beloved of antique dealer impersonators everywhere.

'The books are in the back,' said Tony, indicating two boxes. 'Let's go off and have a coffee, I know a nice place near here where I can park.'

Ha! Just what I'd feared, and expected. No way was I getting in that car.

'There's no need,' I said suavely. 'Quite unnecessary, my dear fellow. I'll just have a look through the boxes right now ...'

'Sorry, it's a no-parking zone. There's a warden coming our way ...'

'I'm sure you can have a word with her,' I said reassuringly, 'I'll only need five or ten minutes ...'

At my side, Malcolm was getting restless. He has a nose for trouble, I thought to myself, good thing I brought him along!

'Get in the fucking car!' he said.

I did, meekly, sitting myself down next to Tony in the front, so that Malcolm could sit in the back and strangle him as necessary. What's that thing called? A garrotte? He could use his scarf.

As we set off on to the ring road, I thought to myself, here I am being taken off to be robbed, at the very least, and the reason I am doing it is because my bodyguard told me to. This was chastening with regard to my backbone, but rather confirmed my idea of his powers.

We drove round for a while, exited after ten minutes, and turned into some sort of open suburban space, carried on down a pitted, single-track road, with a vacant lot on one side, and a single-storey, white-stucco building with a neon sign on the other.

'This is a nice place, run by my family. They make good cappuccino!' said Tony, pulling over to park, then lighting a small Hamlet cigar.

The sign on the restaurant said 'LUIGI'S'.

Opening the door, I walked to the back of the car. 'Let's have a look at the books first. I don't want coffee spilt on them.'

Tony lifted the tailgate of the Volvo, and I took out my list, and a pencil. 'Just give me ten minutes, to check they're all here, and go through them individually.' I'm too often slap-dash, and have more than once purchased books that were later impressions rather than first editions, had missing pages, or had been defaced in some way.

While I ticked off the individual books, and leafed through them, Tony and Malcolm smoked, and talked about football.

I finished the first box, and started on the second. The books were in what booksellers call 'very good' condition, which means not very good – showing signs of wear through-out, but not bad enough to be described as 'good,' which means terrible.

I was mildly disappointed by the two, nearly very good, copies of *Lady Chatterley*, which was first published in 1929 in Italy, in an edition of 1,000 copies signed by Lawrence. (The book wasn't published in England until the Penguin edition, and subsequent trial for obscenity, in 1960.) The books that pleased me most were copies of *Bay – A Book of Poems*, which was published by the small imprint The Beaumont Press, in 1921. As is often the case with finely printed limited editions, the books were sold in three issues: 500 copies, 50 copies signed by DHL, and 25 copies also signed by Lawrence, bound in vellum. Due to a warehouse fire, one of the batch of 50 was actually scarcer (if not as attractive) as one from the batch of 25.

It would have taken a meticulous bookseller a few hours to confirm that all was as it should be, but in fifteen minutes I was satisfied and put the books back into the boot of the Volvo.

'Well,' said Tony, 'have we got a deal?'

'I wish we did,' I said, in my most melancholy voice, 'but the figures don't add up.' I offered to show him my calculations, but he waved the paper away.

'You don't want them?'

'Of course I want them.'

'And?'

'We need to talk about the price ...'

He had said it was non-negotiable, but that is where you start a negotiation, not where you end one.

'How much you want to pay?'

'Seven hundred and fifty pounds.'

He paused for a moment.

'Let's talk over a coffee.'

On the train back to Leamington, which we boarded just past 1.00pm, we sat quietly for a time.

'Thanks for coming, mate,' I said.

'Sure.'

I put the books on the table in front of us, and looked through them for a few minutes.

'We should have stayed for that coffee,' Malcolm said. 'He was a good guy, he seemed a little hurt ...'

'Sorry,' I said. 'I ...'

'Don't worry about it. Can I have a look at the books?'

Barbara's advice, after I returned to Leamington and told her the details, was to deploy this story sparingly and only in sympathetic company. My little adventure didn't reveal me in my best light, nor did it show me, though, in my only light. Carrying all that cash generated a good deal of the anxiety, though it was more characteristic of Woody Allen than of Kierkegaard. I was unconsciously constructing a faux narrative in which I braved dangers, confronted a dragon, returned safely from the hunt with my treasure: a hero, of a modest sort.

If it was obvious to my bodyguard that there was nothing dangerous in my little adventure, it was (almost) apparent to me, too. But if there were no perils, there was less excitement to be had, and that excitement had to be, however unwittingly, ramped up. And so a few narrative adjustments ensued, and grew over time. Was he really called Tony? Did he have an Italian accent? I think so, anyhow he does now. The only glimmering I had of a supposed Mafia connection was when we drew up in front of LUIGI'S, with reality catching up just a little with fantasy.

Like collectors, raconteurs and writers upgrade, making our stories smoother, funnier, more revealing. And if I have long since ceased to collect books – I sold my 160-item Lawrence collection that same year – I'm still addicted to telling stories, telling them again, improving them like my successive first editions of *Sons and Lovers*. The best available copy of that novel, the best possible narration of an adventure, modified, smoothed and improved over years of telling and retelling, getting both more entertaining and (as novelists could tell you) truer with each iteration.

Only three years after purchasing it from Blackwell's, I sold my pride and joy, the dust-wrapped copy of *Sons and Lovers*, when it featured in my first catalogue as a rare book dealer in

1982. It sold for £1,950, and resolved the question of my status with regard to rare books: dealer, not collector.

That's how things started. They got bigger, more interesting, complex and expensive over the next forty years of my career, but the excitement of those early Lawrence purchases and deals still makes me tingle, and tell stories.

2

'The Balls of the Beaver', the Nobel Prize and the Fatwa

I've met a great number of writers, editors and collectors, and like many rare book dealers I've been tempted to become a publisher myself. Such small beer enterprises rarely last very long, for the requisite skills in producing and marketing a new book are ones that we dealers lack. On the other hand, if we take the plunge, we may have some fun, make only a smallish financial loss, and have a ready source of pretty but unsold books that we can give to our friends at Christmas, though we always have more books than friends.

Usually this sort of vanity project is sparked off in some casual way, and a simple desire to branch out, which it is easy to misconceive as creative. In my case, the impulse to do a modest bit of book production came from a series of agreeable interactions with a few writers whom I had met in one way or another in the early 1980s. The first of these was the shrewd and sharp-witted poet Gavin Ewart, from whose library I had been buying some rare books. He had – as most poets do – shelves full of ephemeral poetry publications, for a poet only publishes a full volume very occasionally.

Between full volumes of verse, most poets agree to do limited editions with keen printer/publishers, and why not? Something new, sometimes quite attractively produced, comes into the world, and the poet gets paid a bit, though largely with copies of the pamphlet. As I write, I have recently purchased a large Seamus Heaney collection, which has in it well over a hundred privately printed pamphlets, broadsides, and small volumes. Heaney was just a poet who couldn't say no (except to me), but all poets do similarly, if and when they can. Though such productions are often described as occasional, it would be more accurate to call them frequent. I have a poet friend who has averaged ten a year for the last decade.

I liked and admired Gavin Ewart's work, and inquired if he had something or other that I might publish? He gave a wry smile, and in a few days, I had a typescript of a twelve-line 'rugby song' entitled 'The Balls of the Beaver'. It began:

Castoreum comes from the balls of the Beaver –
Balls of the Beaver – very fine stuff!
A Beaver is truly a big deceiver –
And often found in a lady's muff!

Just the thing! I thought. God only knows why I was content to set the bar so low, though small press publishers often have to take what they can get. Ewart was a widely admired wise-guy, occasionally if improbably mentioned as a possible Poet Laureate. Anyway, the poem was saucy and short, and probably wouldn't cost much to print. (Naïve assumption Number 1 – many to follow.)

I approached Will and Sebastian Carter's Rampant Lions Press in Cambridge, one of the most distinguished English private presses of the time. I'd met Will previously, when he did a slate stone carving of the number 33B, to go on the outside wall of my flat in Chalcot Square in Primrose Hill. The 'B', Will informed me, was in the Gill Sans typeface, shaped (according to its designer) 'like a young girl's buttocks', a subject about which Eric Gill knew altogether too much.

Sebastian was delighted with the commission, and came up with a charming beaver illustration, one of the Henry Holliday adornments to Lewis Carroll's 'The Hunting of the Snark'. We agreed on a distinctly limited edition of 56 copies, of which 50 were bound in paper wrappers, and 6 in a quarter-leather binding and slipcase. But what, Sebastian inquired, and inquired again, was the name of my new press, which would be necessary on the title page?

'Private' presses come in all shapes, sizes, and incarnations. I use the term loosely to indicate what is usually a one-man show, unlikely to make its owner a living: the term 'vanity project' is irresistible. This is a floppy definition, and some imprints are hard to classify, but mine was mine alone, likely to lose money, and done just for the hell of it. Private, and as yet nameless. I had by this time tried dozens of possible appellations, none of which felt anything other than banal, pretentious or witless.

I was then in my final months as a member of the English Department at the University of Warwick, having decided that thirteen years of service was quite enough. I was never comfortable with the institutionalisation of the study of English, and found that it too often undermined my own passion for reading, as well as that of too many of my students. I'd often found myself in conflict with my departmental colleagues, with regard to how and why and when to teach. Being required to be excited about Keats, in my private little room, from 2.00pm–3.00pm on Tuesdays made me feel like a hooker, and I knew how to moan in the right ways at the set times, until I shooed my clients out and ushered the new ones in. It felt phoney, forced, and stale. I revised the prescribed rituals and forms: scheduled open-ended seminars in my own home, offered extra-mural night classes on 'non-literary' subjects like psychoanalysis, clashed with a few of my colleagues on the proper ratio of examined to assessed work, and generally made something of a pain in the arse of myself.

One year I refused to teach our English Poetry course because, in introducing our students to Blake's *Songs of Innocence and Experience*, we were required to employ an anthology which merely printed the words, but didn't reproduce the text on its engraved plate, with script and decoration organically intertwined. The simple text is not the poem, I maintained, and it was on the basis of this assertion that I fell out with my chairman, and publicly and rather ostentatiously refused to teach the course. Blake had set the poems on engraved, illustrated plates, multiple times from their first appearance in 1794. The images are not something extra, however admirable, like Quentin Blake's illustrations for Roald Dahl, they were integral. No plate, no poem, I maintained. My long-suffering colleagues, being intelligent and agreeable, if pragmatic, rather agreed. Bring a copy of the proper text, they said, and show it to your seminar group. And the departmental lecture on *Songs of Innocence and Experience* will use it, too.

I was, however, determined to expose my students to the many, complex and frustrating delights of Blake, so with my colleague Martin Warner, invented a third-year course entitled 'Philosophical Texts', into which Blake's *The Marriage of Heaven and Hell* – also set on engraved illustrated plates – could be slotted. The work contains a plate with a wonderfully ironic self-description by Blake, describing his method of printing:

I was in a Printing house in Hell and saw the method in which knowledge is transmitted from generation to generation.

In the first chamber was a Dragon-Man, clearing away the rubbish from a cave's mouth; within, a number of Dragons were hollowing the cave.

In the second chamber was a Viper folding around the rock and the cave, and others adorning it with gold, silver and precious stones.

In the third chamber was an Eagle with wings and feathers of air, he caused the inside of the cave to be infinite; around were numbers of Eagle-like men who built palaces in the immense cliffs.

In the fourth chamber were Lions of flaming fire raging around and melting the metals into living fluids.

In the fifth chamber were Unnamed forms, which cast the metals into the expanse.

There they were received by Men, who occupied the sixth chamber, and took the forms of books and were arranged in libraries.

The first five chambers are inhabited by symbolic representations of the forces of inspiration, whirling, dangerous, dynamic, unfathomable. And then there is that sixth chamber, in which this creative wildness is tamed, organised, and reduced to the form of books, which sit passively on the shelves of libraries.

The Sixth Chamber Press! That would be the name of my new imprint. I was ever so pleased, though somewhat bemused when the purchasers of the first few books of my new imprint wondered whether the name was a reference to Russian roulette. I explained it again and again, and everyone was rather disappointed to hear my explanation. I soon commissioned a small engraving showing William Blake holding a revolver to his head, but never used it. It seemed to complicate rather than solve the problem.

The dilemma of the publisher's name now solved, things were moving along quite nicely on 'The Balls of the Beaver' – which took longer than I thought it might, and certainly cost more – when a fresh and more exciting opportunity arose, taking me from the ridiculous to the sublime in a single bound volume.

A few years previously, I had been Chairman of the University Faculty of Arts, and in 1981, had the responsibility to look after William Golding, to whom we were awarding the honorary degree of Doctor of Philosophy. It wasn't much fun. Golding hated public exposure, and had long ago given up tours promoting his books, literary festivals, and appearances on TV. Outside of his comfort zone he descended into grump. He lived quietly in a beautiful house in Cornwall, wrote, played the piano, went for walks, ate and drank a lot, and well. He had a select group of local friends whom he trusted, as he felt most comfortable there.

Since my days gobbling up DH Lawrence, I had abjured collecting in favour of dealing. But having met Golding it seemed to me that it would be fun to collect his work, as he might be willing to sign things for me. Some months after coming to Warwick, Golding (reluctantly) agreed to inscribe some of my (newly acquired) first editions of his works, the best of which was a perfect *Lord of the Flies* in a dust wrapper, which I bought for £215, rather a lot at the time. (It would now be worth £15,000.)

We exchanged a few letters, but the relationship, such as it was, began to fizzle out. But then, in 1983, Golding was awarded the Nobel Prize in Literature, frequently and better described as the Nobel Prize *for* Literature. (Golding thought so, too.) Nobel Prize winners are required, when they receive their prize, to give a speech before an audience in Stockholm, and their proud publisher often prints the text for private distribution. My assumption, therefore, was that Faber & Faber would do similarly. I immediately wrote to the publishers to ask if they had such a plan, and was surprised to learn that they did not. 'We don't find publishing such pieces profitable,' I was told. I did not write back to ask whether they had found publishing Golding profitable.

Instead I wrote to Golding, who generously gave me permission to publish the little volume, for which I paid him £500. He immediately understood the 'sixth chamber' allusion, and rather liked it. What he liked less — it was a deal-breaker — was having his Nobel Lecture issued after a poem about a beaver's balls, rather than preceding it, or them. I was happy to agree, and Ewart politely stepped aside. The Nobel Lecture would thus become the first book of my new imprint, and it turned out to be one of the few books of any lasting significance that I was to publish.

I was sufficiently proud of my coup that I then made a bad mistake. I issued the Nobel Lecture, in an edition of 500 copies in brown wrappers, plus 50 signed copies bound in full tan goatskin. Golding was reluctant to sign the copies – he believed, or claimed to believe – that a signature 'defaces' a book, and he had no time for fancy limited editions. Did that mean, I asked, that he regarded books as mere objects of utility? Not at all! 'Of entertainment!' he said. And the entertainment came from the words, not the printing or the format. I made a mental note to talk to him about Blake, but soon and rightly forgot about it.

I had no argument with his dislike of signing, but explained that, if he wouldn't, it made the project unfeasible financially. After a week, he responded that his wife had told him to stop being silly, so he would sign, 'but only slowly'.

The key to running a private press, I'd been advised, was to make sure that the *édition de tête* – the deluxe copies – could be sold at prices sufficient to cover the cost of the entire printing. Sell the 50 signed copies, and the 500 (too many!) were paid for. Thank God for that, because the regular copies were almost impossible to sell at £8.95. I had hundreds of them on my shelves for decades, until I donated a pile of them to Oxfam. They are now worth about £15.

A few years later I complained about the difficulty of selling my ordinary, or 'trade', copies to Charlene Garry, an American bookseller in London who ran the Basilisk Press. Alone of her kind, she actually had a shop, and made an adequate living producing high-end books, some of them facsimiles of similarly high-end books, like the Kelmscott Chaucer and Red Books of Humphrey Repton, as well as colour-plate books about parrots, rhinoceroses, or flowers. They were beautiful and expensive, and sold to (very) rich collectors.

When I told her about my publication of Golding's Nobel Lecture, she laughed.

'You'll learn!' she said, 'You have to obey Charlene's Law!'

I'd never heard of it. Not a lot of people had.

'You can't print too few! You can't charge too much!'

On reflection it made sense. Collectors love rarities, and there will always be a small queue to buy something genuinely scarce, if it is sufficiently attractive. It took me years to learn this lesson, and to find the right formulation. Sixth Chamber books were issued in various numbers and formats, based on my incompetent assessments of the possible market, but few actually lost money.

Years later, when the Sixth Chamber was finished, I formed The Bridgewater Press with my friend the publisher and book collector Tom Rosenthal. His contacts being more extensive than mine, we published books by John Banville, Sebastian Barry, William Boyd, David Lodge, Ian McEwan, and a few other writers. It was from Tom that I finally learnt the right formula: all books must be signed, and limited to: (1) a trade edition of 100 numbered copies, bound in cloth or paper; (2) an intermediate edition of 26 copies lettered A–Z, bound in quarter-leather; (3) a Deluxe Edition, twelve copies numbered I-XII, and bound in full leather, with a slipcase. The Deluxe copies always sold out quickly. Within a couple of years, I had subscribers for seven of them.

Oh, and there's a further little trick beloved of private press proprietors: print a few extra copies, bind them in a distinguishably different version of the Deluxe Binding, and make sure you have printed on the limitation page: 'This is one of __ copies reserved for the publisher.' If this statement is merely added in pen, the market quite rightly neither trusts nor likes it. Too easy to forge extra copies. In 1936, Caresse Crosby's Black Sun Press produced Joyce's *Collected Poems* in an edition of 800 ordinary copies, and a 'special edition', limited to 50 copies signed by Joyce, printed on Japanese vellum, and bound in full black leather. Three further, otherwise identical, 'lettered deluxe copies for private distribution', were delineated A, B and C, and reserved for the author, Crosby herself, and the American publisher. These bear her handwritten description on the limitation leaf, and are unmentioned in the Joyce *Bibliography*. I owned copy B for a time, and found it hard to sell.

My little press was simply staggering from one random opportunity to the next, and the list I was beginning to generate was merely a reflection of whom I'd met recently. It was not very commercial, though the Golding did pretty well because of the signed copies, and the books of poetry sold quickly (if not out) because they were produced in very limited numbers. It was clearly time to do something (that other people) call proactive – a word I detest – I prefer something more homey, like shake a few trees: to write to a few authors whose very names would sell a lot of books. I sent an abject letter of inquiry, asking if I might, please, have something for my Sixth Chamber? All of the writers I approached had, at one point or another, published titles in a private press format. Most were good enough to respond, except for VS Naipaul, which was no surprise. Sebastian Carter suggested that I approach Beckett, with whom he had produced a book, but I was too shy.

Of the writers who said no to my request – Iris Murdoch, Tom Stoppard, Ted Hughes, Seamus Heaney, Philip Larkin – the one that brought me up short was Anthony Powell, whose courteous letter noted that he had a 'horror of writers who produce little odds and ends for the book market'. This high-mindedness was a trifle curious, because he had published a little odd and end only two years previously, entitled *The Empire Revisited*. It was printed by the Cleveland Press, which published only one other book (in 1986) and quickly disappeared, the likely fate of small presses everywhere.

But however tainted by mild hypocrisy, Powell's dismissal rang a bell. I couldn't help feeling similarly. I took little pride in the fact that the Sixth Chamber books were beautifully printed and designed – that was due to Sebastian Carter – but couldn't help but feel that nobody needed or cared very much about them. On a bad day, it began to seem fatuous, and my productions began to tail off. As the 1980s drew to a close, I had added to my list: a short story by Paul Theroux; *A Cluster of Clerihews* by Ewart, a single poem by Peter Redgrove, a short story and a poem by John Updike, and a play by DM Thomas (which was a bad mistake: private press printings of plays never sell). Of these, it was the Updikes that pleased me most. The first (1987) was 'The Afterlife', which had originally been published in the *New Yorker*, and was (to be frank) nothing special. But the poem 'In Memoriam Felis Felis' (1989) is a poignant and funny evocation of the young Updike's visits to a porn movie theatre in Boston. It begins:

The Pussycat on Causeway Street is closed.
Vacant the poster cases that proclaimed
REDHOT, ADULT AND UNINHIBITED.
Dusty and chained the glass doors ...

Happy memories, good dirty fun. But what the text lacked, I felt from the start, was illustrations, though quite what would be suitable was unclear. My friend the architect and book collector Sandy Wilson suggested I contact RB Kitaj – such a good idea! – the only problem being that neither Updike nor Kitaj liked the idea of a collaboration. In August of 1987 Updike wrote to say that he didn't particularly admire Kitaj's work, nor did he believe that words should 'go around playing the handmaiden to present fashionable painters'. If that weren't enough to put me off, Kitaj, while proclaiming that Updike was one of his favourite writers, said he had neither the time nor the desire to illustrate one of his works, being 'very reclusive'.

Not a match made in Heaven? I persevered, and eventually Updike capitulated, and Kitaj kindly gave me carte blanche to go to The Marlborough Gallery (who represented him) to look through their files of his images, and to 'use anything you like'. I found a painting of louche young people that might go on the cover of the book, a painting of a man peering intently at something, a picture of a movie theatre marquee with the word 'frantic' and some nudes below it, and most appropriately a full-frontal drawing of a spread-legged nude woman, to go opposite Updike's lines: 'The screen would be ablaze with private parts ... Whose only point was reached recurrently at bright pink junctures flecked with pubic hair.' Right up Updike's alley: he once published a book entitled *Cunts*. I sent the images to him, and he agreed that they fit 'remarkably well'. I was more pleased than I'd been with any of my former books, because I'd had a genuine if minor creative role in putting the text and images together.

As the 1980s drew to a close, The Sixth Chamber Press (like Pope's alexandrine) was 'like a wounded snake, that drags its slow length along', and I was increasingly bored by looking at a garage full of unsold books, becoming damper and less saleable by the week ... month ... year ... years. And then two fortuitous things happened, and all of a sudden I had a hit on my hands. The first was that I became friendly with Salman Rushdie, with whom I occasionally played ping-pong, and the second, which it would be quite wrong to characterise as 'luck', was the coming of the Fatwa.

Rushdie was an accomplished novelist and essayist, a terrific short-story writer, and an articulate and persuasive commentator on, well, almost anything. I admired and liked him enormously, and was delighted when he began a relationship with my friend and former student Lizzy West, at that time personal assistant to Salman's editor, Liz Calder. Salman generously gave permission to print two of his stories, which had previously been published in magazines: 'The Prophet's Hair' and 'The Free Radio'. He suggested, too, that they might be illustrated by his friend, the Indian painter Bhupen Khakhar (later to have a retrospective at the Tate), who provided wood blocks for five woodcuts and three linocuts. This led to a book of 72 signed copies – titled *Two Stories* – in designer bindings by Romilly Saumarez Smith. The twelve special copies had a full leather binding, slipcase, and an extra set of the eight prints in an enclosed folder, each signed by Khakhar. It was by far the most lavish and beautiful book I had published.

Rushdie had won the Booker in 1981 with *Midnight's Children*, and been shortlisted in 1983 for *Shame*, but in the rare book market, only the first edition of *Midnight's Children* fetched strong prices, and it wasn't clear whether I'd be able to sell the sixty ordinary copies.

The sheets were printed by Sebastian Carter, the eight blocks revealed their stunning images, Romilly submitted designs for the binding: the book was coming together smoothly, and the only production delay was that we had to get Bhupen's signature on his prints. It might have been possible to courier them back and forth, but preferable to get them to him in person. Salman had no plans to visit India, nor did I. And then, on 14 February 1988, the Ayatollah Khomeini issued his Fatwa in response to *The Satanic Verses*, condemning Rushdie – as well as 'his editors and publishers' – to death. At first, no one quite knew what to make of this, it being the first time radical Islamism had entered the West. But we soon found out. Copies of the novel were burnt, and Rushdie henceforth had to lead a careful, largely secluded and heavily guarded life.

He had always insisted upon his right to take on big topics, and to offend if necessary, openly, intelligently, and with artistic integrity. And all of a sudden hordes of screaming protesters were burning (but not reading) his book and screaming for him to be murdered. In England! Was it dangerous to bring those sheets for Bhupen's signature? I hoped it wasn't, because my friend Geordie Grieg, then literary editor of the *Sunday Times*, was soon off on a trip to India, and happy to carry the printed sheets in his suitcase. He came back unscathed with the sheets ready to print, speaking warmly of his meeting with Khakhar, who found the whole business rather exciting.

On publication in 1989, the book was greatly admired by all who saw it, some of whom even bought a copy. (I tell the story of the launch party in *Tolkien's Gown*). The twelve copies were soon gone, and the sixty sold regularly if slowly.

The Sixth Chamber Press drew to a close much as it had begun, with an odd conjunction of titles and of images: from pubic hair to 'Prophet's Hair'. I'd had enough, really, but private press publishers are always open to a new opportunity. In 1991 I used the imprint to publish a couple of books, but as they were not designed by Sebastian, I never thought of them as fully-fledged Sixth Chamber items. The first (in 1991) was by my former colleague George O'Brien, whose *The Village of Longing* was a prize-winning memoir of his childhood, which we offered in a signed edition of twenty-five copies; the second was Vikram Seth's *A Suitable Boy* (1993), for which I bought sheets from the publisher, and had them bound at Smith, Settle Bindery in Yorkshire. Both signed issues (100 and 26) sold out immediately, as the book was a hot tip for the Booker, though it didn't make the short list.

In 1994 the last genuine book of the Press was printed and designed by Sebastian Carter, according to my brief: *go a little bit crazy!* The resulting pamphlet of sixteen pages is printed in a variety of coloured inks in a series of different formats, angles and postures. 'Such a lot of fun!' said Sebastian. It was titled *Gekoski: the First Fifty Years*, and given as a gift to fifty friends in (self) honour of my fiftieth birthday. It was partly a whimsical take on Blake's 'Proverbs of Hell': 'Wisdom is not accumulated, but shed' . . . that sort of thing.

The book began:

As I detest writing, I've done this,
for my own amusement, in a kind of shorthand.
I send this foolish bit of self-indulgence in the hope
that it will recall me to friends unseen for too long,
as well as serving as an unnecessary irritant
to those I see more frequently.

And on the final page there was this:

Attentive readers may believe they can discern
beneath these random frivolities and mock apercus
the clear outline of a philosophy of life.

They are wrong.

I have twice seen copies of this pamphlet offered at £250 by rare book dealers. If you suppose this says anything about the market for Rick Gekoski, you are wrong. But it tells us a great deal about the value of books designed and printed by the masterful Sebastian Carter.

3

Dealing with Ted Hughes

RA Gekoski – Modern First Editions
Catalogue 6, Spring, 1985, item 168.

(PLATH, SYLVIA). Fitzgerald, F Scott, The Great Gatsby,
New York, (1925). Sylvia Plath's copy, with her bookplate,
underlinings, and annotations. Twelve holograph comments
(about 60 words) appear to be observations for teaching
purposes ... her underlinings locate observations, and more
particularly images, in the novel that make it seem remarkably
similar to her later poetry ... paying particular attention to
colours, visual images, states of the weather, and psychological
gloom. £575

I'm surprised, reading my former catalogue description, that I
didn't mention the (1931) Rockwell Kent bookplate that was
pasted in by Plath. This wood engraving of a gigantic woman
dwarfing the landscape – powerful, hermaphroditic, and (curiously) literary – seems, in the Plath context ... well, significant.

You learn a lot from owning such a book. I'm not thinking

of what you can discover from these annotations, which is a lot – no, what I mean is that sometimes you think you own a book, then you don't, then you do again.

An explanation is in order. I bought it in 1984 in New York for $500, at the time a little over £200. It was love at first sight. I can still recall how thrilling it was to hold in my hand, to leaf through the pages. Sexy. That's the word dealers use for items that make you tingle.

It eventually sold to Professor Matthew J Bruccoli, a fanatical Fitzgerald collector, whose extensive collection would one day be gifted to the University of South Carolina, where he taught. A native of the Bronx, Matt had reinvented himself as a natty man of the Gatsby world, with a bristly moustache, flamboyant wardrobe and vintage red Mercedes. He loved showing off his treasures, and the lust they caused in other collectors. One of whom, Maurice Neville of Santa Barbara, California, was so taken by Bruccoli's copy of the first edition of *For Whom the Bell Tolls*, inscribed by Hemingway to Fitzgerald, that he kept raising his offer to buy it from generous to outlandish. No luck.

After making a few discreet inquiries worthy of Sam Spade, Neville flew to South Carolina and invited Matt out to lunch at a carefully chosen restaurant.

'That's not a very good place,' said Matt, who loved his grub. 'Why not let me do the reservation? I'll take you ...'

'Humour me,' said Neville. As predicted, the food was indifferent, and by the end of the meal the normally loquacious Professor was in no mood for further chat. When they left, Neville took his arm, and said, 'Turn right.' Some way down the street was a luxurious car dealership with the sign

'JAGUAR' (Americans pronounce it '*Jag-war*'). Bruccoli scratched his head, they entered the showroom and a sleek salesman – English! – greeted them.

'Ah, Professor Bruccoli, such an honour to see you, sir.'

Neville knew that owning a resplendent new Jaguar, with all the trimmings, was Bruccoli's most potent fantasy. And he was there to offer its fulfilment.

'Choose any model you like, add anything you want to the specifications. It's yours! All I want is that damn book!'

Bruccoli looked genuinely chagrined, walked round the showroom, opened doors and peered in at the wood and leather, sniffed, closed his eyes, sighed.

'Nice move!' he said. 'Good try!'

Years later, Bruccoli liked to claim that his neck was still cricked from looking backwards ruefully as he walked away from his temptation.

'Like Orpheus!' he said.

Plath's marginalia and underlinings, perhaps from her under-graduate years at Smith College, are in most instances unre-markable, but in others precocious, almost prescient about the trials to come. Looking through the annotations, you can infer the personality behind them – assiduous, ambitious, powerful, and above all self-referring. In her mind, perhaps, the novel might have been titled *The Great Daisy*.

Plath's marginal note: '*l'ennui*' – where Daisy describes herself ('I've been everywhere and seen everything and done everything') – is noteworthy because Sylvia soon composed a poem of that title. More interesting is her underlining of the passage ending '... the best thing a girl can be in this world, a beautiful little fool'. Plath was certainly beautiful, and palpably no fool, but her struggles against the sterile, prevailing images of womanhood in the 1950s were constant, and she only began to find her way, and her most confident voice, when she left America to study at Cambridge. There, of course, she met Ted Hughes, and I wonder how much that tumultuous relationship might be prefigured by her notes? Next to the Gatsby lines '... the sacredness of the vigil. So I walked away and left him standing there in the moonlight – watching over nothing,' Plath has written: 'knight waiting outside – dragon goes to bed with princess'. (There is a later Plath poem which seems related, entitled 'The Princess and the Goblins'.)

The dragon is associated in Christian theology with darkness and the devil, but the image of the dragon is (perhaps surprisingly) absent from Hughes' poems. It can be found in his children's book *The Iron Man*, in which a 'space-bat-angel-dragon' appears from outer space, and explains itself: "'Haven't you heard of the music of the spheres?" asked the dragon. "It's the music that space makes to itself. All the spirits inside all the stars are singing. I'm a star spirit. I sing, too. The music of the spheres is what makes space so peaceful."'

That's a very bardic dragon, that one, at once dangerous and poetic. You can imagine the star-struck Sylvia, on first meeting Ted at that fabled Cambridge drinks party – she kissed and bit his neck until he bled – murmuring, 'Just what I was waiting for,' or (as she later described it) 'He had sex as strong as it comes.'

These are tenuous prefigurations, and I would need more time to flesh them out to see if they're justified. But that's what happens when you read someone's marginalia, you're peeping over their shoulder, reading the book with them. It makes you feel more privileged than you have a right to feel, as if you are actually inside the reading process. I love dealing in books with extensive marginalia, though there are surprisingly few of them about. Most readers are fastidious about writing in their books. When my friends discover that I scribble all over mine, they are often censorious. Apparently I'm defacing the book, whereas what I think I'm doing is entering into a relationship with its author. If I can't write 'wonderful!' or 'bullshit!' in a margin, I feel excluded, and silenced. Coleridge, of course, is my guide and mentor in such relationships. He was a compulsive annotator, and many of his occasional comments have made their way into the received critical literature, like his 'motiveless malignity' marginal description of Iago.

Some writers read with a pencil in hand, and often put ticks in the margins, or underline a passage, but seldom more. When I encounter such books, I get very excited and almost always overvalue, and overprice them. I once owned John Kennedy Toole's paperback copy of *Finnegans Wake*, which he used while studying at Columbia, with hundreds of words of annotation over the first eighty pages. Presumably he, like many readers, gave up at that point. My father's copy, curiously, has annotations that close at much the same point. I suspect the reason is not that the text gets boring or more difficult at that passage, but that the human spirit can only bear a certain amount of Finneganing. My customers couldn't abide any; I catalogued the Toole/Joyce book enthusiastically, failed to find a buyer, and it sat on my shelves for years. Such experiences test the respect that my customers usually enjoy.

After I returned to London with Sylvia's *Gatsby*, I showed it off to my fellow dealers, hugging it to my breast, muttering 'My precious', like Gollum. It soon featured in my next catalogue, and the day after it was posted I received a letter, dated 13 May from Carol Hughes, second wife of Ted:

Dear Rick

Thank you for sending us your most recent catalogue, though we are curious about item 168 – Sylvia's Great Gatsby. *That was part of her library, which of course remained with Ted after her death. It was stolen a few years ago from Court Green – before her archive and library went to Smith in the States.*

The problem is the next step to take – and we would be grateful for your help, though I realise it puts you somewhat in the middle.

Do please get in touch, Ted feels we should take some action fairly soon.

We look forward to hearing from you,

Yours,

Carol Hughes

Though couched politely, this sounded a tad threatening. I have no idea what 'step' or 'action' Ted was contemplating, and had no desire to find out.

I responded the next day to explain the provenance of the book (as far as I then knew it) and to apologise for my inadvertent part in its recent history. Though there was scant chance of getting my money back from the dealer from whom I'd bought it, it was clear to me what needed to happen next:

*'... you and Ted own the book, and should have it back.
Fortunately, it hasn't sold yet ... I'm sorry to have been involved
in buying it, but of course, when you deal in as much association
material as I do, this sort of thing is bound to happen now and
again. Thank you for writing to me so promptly.'*

A few days later, I drove to Devon from Warwickshire to give
the book back to Carol and Ted, and arrived at tea-time, as I
had suggested, after a tedious four-hour journey. I knocked at
the door, which was soon half-opened. A face peered out.

'Oh, yes, thank you.'

A hand reached out to take the book. The door closed.

A couple of days later, I had a letter from Carol thanking
me for returning the book ('that was a very kind gesture'),
telling me that over the years 'quite a few items "walked" from
Court Green – part of life I suppose'. I heard from Ted a
month later: 'Your magnanimous gesture, returning to us
Sylvia's copy of *The Great Gatsby*, startled me somewhat. I
hope I shall be able to do you a good turn at some point.'

I wasn't satisfied that this was the end of the matter, and
made some further inquiries, after which I solved the provenance problem: the route was almost predictable. Which was
more likely: that someone had stolen one of Sylvia's books
from Court Green, the Hugheses' house in Devon, or that
someone with access to those shelves had carried it off to
read, and never returned it? I asked the dealer from whom I'd
purchased it where he'd got it. From another dealer. Where'd
he get it? At first he didn't want to say, citing client confidentiality. But when told the whole story, he revealed that he'd
purchased it from Sylvia's mother, Aurelia – reputedly a

difficult woman, but hardly a book thief. She'd probably taken it to read on the plane on her way home after a visit to England.

I wrote to Ted to convey this news, and heard from him a few weeks later, still grateful, if a bit rueful at having to give the book back to me: 'It was very good of you to send me *The Great Gatsby*. I've been intending to return it to you . . . There's no reason at all why you should lose by it, anyway, whatever route it took.' The book was still demonstrably his property, and it was generous of him to cede possession.

I met Ted a couple of times subsequent to this. We were introduced by his sister Olwyn, with whom I had a long friendship. It was impossible not to feel impressed and slightly diminished by him, he was cloaked in charisma, talked in short sentences, and often generated silences which, if you filled them too anxiously, made you feel a ninny. I don't know if he was aware of how intimidating he was, or if he played it up. Though many of his friends described times in which he could be good company, often on a riverbank, many others found him overpowering in a manner too easily parodied. Melvyn Bragg compared him to Heathcliff; when Hughes did a poetry reading at Hull, Larkin wrote to a friend that 'I was in the chair, providing a sophisticated, insincere, effete, and gold-watch-chained alternative to his primitive, forthright, virile, leather-jacketed persona.' This thrusting potency was sufficient to cause unease amongst his fellow men, and not a few of his lovers, many of whom, by frequent accounts, rose from his bed more shaken than stirred.

Within a couple of years, Ted made good on his promise to do me 'a good turn'. In March of 1988, he told our mutual friend Roy Davids, Head of the Book Department at Sotheby's, that he would be glad to inscribe some of his books for me. I chose a few and gave them to Roy. When they came back, the inscriptions were generous, and thoughtful, not the unadorned 'with best wishes' pap with which authors – I do it sometimes – often sign their books. No, in each was a bit of poetry, seemingly created on the spot, for I could not find Hughes had used the same words anywhere else.

On a first edition of his first book, *The Hawk in the Rain* (1957), Ted wrote:

> For Rick
> 'The Morning Hour
> has gold in its mouth'
> Best Wishes
> Ted Hughes
> 29th March 1988.

Similarly, he embellished proof copies of *Wodwo* (1967): 'The new boat finds the old rocks'; and *Crow* (1970): 'When the wolf grows old the crow rides him' – both of which said 'Greetings', which seemed a tad warmer than 'Best wishes'. I was delighted by the generosity and creative resonance of these inscriptions, and wrote fulsomely to say so.

The second magnanimous gesture on Ted's part was to offer to sell me for £4,000 (through Roy Davids) his copy of the American first edition of Sylvia's first book, *The Colossus* (1962) with a wonderful inscription from her to him. Ted frequently sold material from Court Green, either en bloc (Sylvia's library to Smith College) or single items of books or manuscripts. But previously this had been done discreetly, usually through Roy or via Olwyn, or occasionally through the rare book trade.

I was stunned and delighted to be able to buy a book of this resonance. I catalogued it in 1992, citing this most marvellous inscription, combining references to both her husband and her father: 'FOR TED "Of whom Colossus and Prince Otto learn their craft and art." With love, Sylvia.' I priced it at £9,500. If I gave my customary 20 per cent discount to a buyer, that would leave me with £7,600, or slightly less than the hoped for doubling up. It never occurred to me that this would be misunderstood, but it was. The day after the catalogue came out, I heard not from Ted, but from Roy.

'Ted is furious!' he said.

'Why's that?'

'He thinks dealers only get 10 per cent,' said Roy, who knew better. Ted did, too, as he had sold books into the rare book trade in his early years as a poet.

'Then you should explain to him that we often have to give discounts when we sell books, that cataloguing costs a lot, and that sometimes books don't sell. He's used to dealing with auctioneers, who never have to put up their own money, and who charge both the buyer and the seller. He could have given the book to me on consignment, and I would only have charged him 20 per cent, but then he wouldn't have had immediate cash in hand ...'

'I've explained that,' said Roy laconically.

Both of us knew that he had not, and would not. Ted was his trusted friend and client, but their relations were by no means equal. Roy's role was to be agreeable, and to agree.

When he once stepped outside this box to warn Ted that one of his more obscure laureate poems about the royals 'might lose people', the opinion was unwelcome. So he was hardly likely to defend me or my normal business practices.

I'd paid Ted's price, without haggling. Once I bought the book, it was mine. Surely I could then price it however I wished? That's how I felt at the time, and it strikes me retrospectively as naïve: just because I understand what I am doing, it doesn't mean it would be clear to someone outside the loop. I might have avoided any misunderstanding by selling the book privately rather than through a catalogue. But being a rare book dealer means putting your best wares on the table: it confirms you're a player, and it's likely to attract more material, and more eager customers.

Except that it didn't. My (previously Ted's) copy of *The Colossus* was more admired than purchased. People loved the inscription, and wanted to know the back story. But it sat on my shelves for many months – perhaps it (or I) was too sophisticated, or my price was bullish – and I eventually sold it to a canny American collector for £5,000, at which price, taking into account all overheads and expenses, I might have made a small profit. (In 2002, the book sold at Christie's for $38,850 – a price I would happily pay for it today).

The problem with Ted was upsetting. I hate it when Poet Laureates get mad at me. I suggested to Roy that I might write to tell Ted the final price I'd received, but his answer was 'DON'T!'

In the following years I sold a few things on Ted's behalf to Emory University, which had a strong collection of twentieth-century poetry, and where the young Head of Manuscripts,

Steve Enniss, was keen to build their Hughes holdings. In 1995, Davids began to offer them significant individual manuscripts at prices that Enniss found resistible: 'No, we would not buy the manuscript, but if you ever had anything more substantial to offer let me know.' Enniss goes on to tell the story: 'I thought no more of the conversation until a year later when Roy phoned to tell me he was representing Ted Hughes in the sale of his archive and to ask whether Emory would be interested in purchasing the entire collection. I was stunned. Hughes was the leading English poet of his generation; for more than a decade he had held the post of Poet Laureate, and he was known to be an exceedingly private person, one who shrank from interviews, readings, and other forms of public exposure. His complete archive was now being offered to a young American university whose chief virtue was an unbridled ambition.'

In 1997 the deal was completed for what Davids had called 'the complete collection'. Of course it was not complete in the sense that it included everything that Hughes had written: in the early years he regularly sold poetic manuscripts (which, he retrospectively regretted, he had sold cheaply), including those of poems that he regarded as his 'freshest' work. But what remained was close to a hundred linear feet of manuscript drafts, letters, reviews and clippings, snapshots, and other bits and pieces of his writing life. Emory were delighted with the acquisition, and happy to accede to the contractual condition that the sale excepted papers relating to Hughes' 'current projects', the clear implication, as Enniss understood it, being that Emory were purchasing (virtually) all available material produced up to the date of the contract, and that they would have first refusal on material created after that date.

Hughes died the next year, so there would presumably have been very little material left to complete the Emory holdings. So it came as something of a surprise when, in 2008, Carol Hughes sold the residual material from Hughes' literary estate to the British Library, which described it as: 'over 465 files, volumes and oversize items, the archive includes literary drafts, correspondence, notebooks, professional papers and diaries'. It also included Hughes' fishing journals and many personal diaries that recorded his increasingly vivid dreams and reflections on his family and past. As well, of course, as the poems about his relations with Sylvia, which were composed over a period of some twenty-eight years, during which time Hughes hesitated to publish them, regarding them as 'too raw and unguarded'. So the eventual publication of *Birthday Letters* (1999), his long-awaited poetic account of his relations with Sylvia, might be regarded as the culmination of 'work in progress'. It was greeted with rapturous praise.

The many drafts of the eighty-eight poems and ancillary material were not included in the Emory transaction. Indeed, Enniss tells me, he was never shown or told about them, since they fell under the (perhaps insufficiently interrogated) contractual rubric that excluded ongoing work. But a large amount of other material, which was by no means work in progress, was included in the 2008 sale. Had Davids and Hughes been parsimonious with the truth? Enniss certainly thought so: 'I felt we had been hoodwinked. There were two archives all along, that was their plan.' A heated exchange of letters in the *TLS* ensued, in which both Davids and Enniss claimed the high ground.

Emory had, of course, the contractual right of first refusal on what Enniss calls the 'additional' material, but the price of £500,000 was more, even, than they had paid for the original, and much deeper, archive. They demurred. The British Library hadn't been offered the original archive in 1997, since Roy Davids had assured Hughes that a British institution would never pay as much as the right American one. So when the new – or 'second' – archive was offered, they felt they had to buy it. In general, libraries do not like broken archives: it's best for papers to be housed in one institution, but this was an exception worth making. Ted Hughes had been Poet Laureate from 1984 until his death in 1998. The Hughes–Plath material was irresistible: their relationship was, by this time, of almost mythical status, they were the most compelling literary couple since Robert and Elizabeth Barrett Browning. The papers would be consulted, quoted and argued about voraciously for generations. Best to buy them without worrying too much about the bifurcation of the archive.

I'd no further contact with Ted before his death, but it was not the end of our relations, which extended, if I might put it like this, beyond the grave. This is where his sister Olwyn, literary agent to the Estate of Sylvia Plath, came in, not like some mythic chthonic force, though sometimes she rather suggested one, but because my Hughes dealings now went through her. Olwyn was a remarkable woman, with her fair share of the family charisma and power, a wonderful companion over bottles of wine and a long dinner. Shrewd, sardonic and indomitable, she had a wonderful memory, especially for slights and revealing gossip. She became Ted's gateway to the world, arranging contracts and details for the sales of his books, and publishing, through her Rainbow Press, a number of his titles in finely printed and bound limited editions. I bought a lot of them.

Olwyn made it her job – prompted by Ted, or perhaps only with his slight nod of the head – to curate, to edit and to rewrite, the story of Ted's relations with Sylvia. Appointed as Plath's literary executor, she took on the role of guardian at the gates, armed and dangerous, impassable. Not only was she protective towards Ted, but more particularly of her niece and nephew, Frieda and Nicholas, whom she wished to shield from the growing cultural tendency for young women to demonise their father, and to see Sylvia as the innocent victim of his abuse and infidelity: hadn't Sylvia committed suicide after Ted's affair with Assia Wevill? And then Assia did, too, killing her daughter at the same time!

When the poet Anne Stevenson was working on *Bitter Fame*, her *Life of Sylvia Plath*, Olwyn insisted on reading each draft, making comments and revisions on a sentence-by-sentence basis, dragging the story into line with her version of it: that Sylvia, however talented, was a thoroughly difficult and narcissistic woman, and that Ted had supported and encouraged her consistently. After all, Olwyn would say with a grimace, it was Sylvia who had twice destroyed Ted's working manuscripts! (This sounds more horrific than it probably was: Ted had a stupendous memory – it is said he knew all of Shakespeare by heart – and it's likely that he could reconstruct all the poems that had been destroyed. Sylvia knew this.)

Pity poor Anne Stevenson, an excellent poet and potentially a very fine biographer. Olwyn referred to her as 'that silly little woman', and saw it as her job constantly to review and to redirect her judgements, to interrogate her insights and prose. Anthony Thwaite's review of *Bitter Fame* in the *LRB* catches the problem perfectly, and expresses his exasperation at what he clearly felt was an artistic imposition:

> *Anne Stevenson, against the odds, has written a decent and intelligent book . . . But* Bitter Fame *carries its marks of constraint and difficulty as well. A prefatory Author's Note acknowledges 'a great deal of help from Olwyn Hughes, literary agent to the Estate of Sylvia Plath. Ms Hughes's contributions to the text have made it almost a work of dual authorship.'*
>
> *The proof copy I was originally sent phrases it rather differently: 'This biography of Sylvia Plath is the result of a three-year dialogue between the author and Olwyn Hughes, agent to the Plath Estate. Ms Hughes has contributed so liberally to the text that this is, in effect, a work of joint authorship. I have in particular to acknowledge her contribution to the biographical material in the last four chapters.'*

Well, Olwyn gave good duress, and it was often diverting when others were at the receiving end of it. But, eventually it was me who was under fire. The occasion for this break in relations involved a panther, or perhaps it was a jaguar, they're much the same.

Somehow, it figured: the omens were in place. The fourth book that Ted inscribed for me in 1988 was a copy of *Poetry from Cambridge 1952–1954*, which was edited by Karl Miller and published by Oscar Mellor's Fantasy Press in 1955. Ted contributed three poems to the volume, one of which (on page 29) was 'The Jaguar'. Hughes lived for a time near Regent's Park Zoo, which he often visited, and though this poem about a caged animal recalls Rilke's poem of the same title, it's more fun to think of it as a youthful self-portrait of the artist as a young beast:

> *. . . slavering jaw hanging,*
> *The crazed eye satisfied to be blind in fire,*
> *By the bang of blood in the brain deaf the ear . . .*

Beneath the poem – rather than either of the (tamer) other poems – Hughes signed his name, adding 'for Rick', with the date. Retrospectively it feels a little spooky.

At much the same period that 'The Jaguar' was composed, Plath wrote 'The Pursuit' – only a couple of days after meeting and biting Ted – comparing him to a panther, and making herself his prey:

> *There is a panther stalks me down:*
> *One day I'll have my death of him;*
> *His greed has set the woods aflame,*
> *He prowls more lordly than the sun.*

You'd hardly need to consult your Ouija board or read your horoscopes (they did both) to see trouble coming.

Four years after Sylvia's death, when Frieda was at school in Devon, Ted went to the arts and crafts room with his little girl to make some animal figures out of clay. Hers was an owl, and her father moulded two images of a jaguar in clay, glazed them black and fired them. He gave one to Olwyn – which later got broken – and one to his brother Gerald in Australia. In 2011, Gerald sent his jaguar to his sister, in the hope that she could raise some money selling it. She rang me, and soon enough I was in her sitting room in Dartmouth Park, looking at the remarkable sculpture.

'It's amazing!' I said, holding it carefully, feeling the modelling of the sinews, the sheer power of it.

'Did he do a lot of this sort of thing?'

'Only the two. Can you sell it? How much can you get for it?'

'Of course I can,' I said. (I later discovered that Ted had made plasticine models of animals since childhood. It was a relief to learn that he couldn't do such skilful work at a first go.)

'Let me think, and work out how to find the best buyer. I'll get back to you ...'

'Get a move on!' said Olwyn sharply. 'Gerald's ninety, and he's completely broke.'

Bemused, I went back to my Primrose Hill flat to see if I could work out how to market the piece. And, crucially, at what price? How did one contextualise it, what were the comparators? Was it worth more than Hughes' first book? Of course. More than a manuscript poem or letter? Probably.

Art created by writers is not an uncommon category. There are numerous paintings by DH Lawrence, Lawrence Durrell, Henry Miller, Kenneth Patchen, and others, and many writers drew well and frequently: Hardy, Conrad, Wells, and indeed Sylvia Plath and Ted Hughes. But I couldn't think of any parallel to Ted's ceramic figure. The problem in pricing it was not that it was unique – any damn fool can whip up an animal out of clay – but that it was good. If it had been terrible it would have been worth a few hundred pounds; but it was special, even if you didn't know who made it.

Pricing depends upon a market. Book collectors are not in general imaginative: it's hard even to sell most of them a letter by, or photograph of, their favourite author. No, what I needed was either a research institution with a major Hughes collection, or, not a Hughes collector, but a Hughes nut. I knew a couple of each.

Drum up interest! Big it up! As I often did when I had something of particular interest, I rang the arts journalist Dalya Alberge, who was immediately entranced by the story, and within a few days had interviewed Olwyn, and begun an article, with a picture of the jaguar, ready for publication in the *Guardian*.

A few days before its publication, I visited Olwyn to discuss the price, and suggested £2,500, though it seemed high to me.

She laughed scornfully. 'That's ridiculous,' she said. 'I want five thousand pounds!'

'In hand?'

'Absolutely!'

'Tell me how you came to that valuation?'

She laughed again, and turned down the corners of her mouth. 'It's what it's worth! Do you want to sell it or don't you?'

Well, I certainly wanted to offer it, but minimally I would have to price it at £7,500, which wouldn't leave any wiggle room after the usual discount and haggling. Better hung for a robber than a poacher: I priced it at £10,000. But I was unwilling to put it in a catalogue: if I offered the jaguar publicly, it would make me look foolish, and greedy. For that price, at that time, you could buy a Henry Moore maquette. But Olwyn was a friend, we'd done a load of business, and she'd been generous in the past, so I could offer the dratted jaguar discreetly to a few possible customers. After all, I could hide behind the phrase, when my price was greeted with incredulity, 'It's on consignment ...' Don't blame me, mate.

I offered the piece, first, to Steve Enniss who was building the Hughes collection at Emory. I had sold him dozens of books, and a great many manuscripts and letters, and this new ceramic piece would stretch the boundaries of the collection, and make a fabulous item in a vitrine at a Ted Hughes exhibition. I emailed Steve with an image of the jaguar and a fulsome description of it.

He responded quickly.

'Not for us, thanks for offering.'

Next port of call was Roy Davids, Ted's buddy, and a passionate Hughes collector, with many manuscripts, plus an ink portrait of Ted done by Sylvia.

I got the same response, and I got it again and again, from other Hughes collectors, some of whom could see the point of buying it, but thought the price unusually aggressive.

I relayed the news to Olwyn.

'Never mind, love,' she said. 'They're idiots. I'll sell it myself.'

Of course, this cut out the middle man, and brought the price right down to the £5,000 that she wanted in the first place. To my surprise, she soon placed it with a Yorkshire schoolmaster who was a Hughes fanatic, and had loved the piece from the first, but resisted my initial price. Clever him.

When the *Guardian* article by Dalya appeared, it quoted Olwyn extensively about the jaguar, elicited an excited opinion from Jonathan Bate, who was writing a biography of Hughes, and ended with a quote from me, the agent offering it for sale: 'It seems to me powerful, dark, sexual, predatory, which are terms that have frequently been used to describe Ted Hughes. But it also seems to me to have quite a lot of inwardness and feeling. The head is low rather than high. It doesn't look like an animal that's attacking.'

That seemed to me a fair comment, but it certainly didn't to Olwyn. I had a phone call that morning: 'How dare you call Ted "predatory" . . . he was nothing of the sort!'

'Olwyn, dear, I didn't! But other people have, and after all a jaguar is a predator . . .'

'Ted was pursued by women, they were all over him! They were throwing their panties in his face!'

We let the topic, and him, rest . . . if not in peace, at least in abeyance.

Olwyn later sold her extraordinary group of letters from her adored brother for about half of what they were worth. She never asked my opinion.

4

The Third Woman: Yvonne
Cloetta and Graham Greene

She was bang on time, alas. Twelve sharp, as she entered the
modest one-bedroom flat overlooking the Marina in Antibes,
the sea glinting as if appropriated from a Raoul Dufy painting, the room bathed in light on that summer day in 1989. I
made my way from perusing the bookshelves, and Graham
made the introductions: 'Yvonne, Rick. Rick, Yvonne.'

She was about as happy to see me as I was her. Greene's lover
and sometime companion for thirty years, Yvonne Cloetta
lived a few miles away in Juan les Pins with her husband Jacques,
when he was home from working in Africa, an arrangement
that gave her plenty of time to spend with Graham. A petite
Frenchwoman in her early fifties, with the perfect hair that
goes with the type, she wore a pale lemon silk blouse, and
leather trousers which fit her snugly and to everyone's advantage. *Chic*, I thought, *très chic*, a failure of both attentiveness and
vocabulary that was understandable if not forgivable.

I'd spent the last half-hour scanning the heavily laden
bookshelves avidly, with carte blanche from my host to pull

off and make an offer to buy any books that caught my eye. So far I'd found a beautiful little illustrated Fanny Hill (the second edition, with coloured plates), a first edition of *At Swim Two Birds*, which was dedicated by Flann O'Brien to Greene (but lacked a personal inscription), and – how terrific! – a number of books inscribed to Greene by Evelyn Waugh.

'I think I'll keep those,' he said. Noting my disappointment (little escaped the penetration of those dewy Wedgwood-blue eyes) he added, 'but you're welcome to go to my flat in Paris, if you can be bothered. There are lots of books there, including my own copies of my own books. I don't need those anymore.'

That thought alone was sufficient to rouse me from my treasure hunting to join Graham and Yvonne over a bottle of wine before we went off to lunch at La Colombe d'Or, in Saint-Paul-de-Vence. We had business to discuss. The previous night, sitting on the single bed in my cramped hotel room just up the road, I had read all of Greene's 123 letters to her, which he'd told me that Yvonne wished to sell.

The letters gave me a clear idea, though not a deep one, of who she was, and how Greene treated and regarded her. What they couldn't tell me, of course, was who she was not. By the time I understood the implications of this, it was too late. They were persons, she and Graham, whom I didn't understand sufficiently until I later read about them, and filled in the gaps. Perhaps not even then: as Norman Sherry was ruefully to admit, even after writing the 2,200 pages of his bloated biography of Greene, he hadn't entirely 'caught' his subject. Perhaps biographical subjects are different from fish.

The topic of the sale of the letters was best approached

after a few more drinks. We drove to the restaurant for lunch, and were seated on the terrace overlooking the sea. The lunch itself was adequate demonstration of the *mot* that the better the view, the worse the food. There was no need for the chef even to try, not there! But the fish was fresh, and it's hard to ruin *pommes frites et salade*.

Graham was spotted by a diner, who wandered over with a camera, and asked politely if he might take a photo. I slicked my hair back, adjusted my chair to just the right angle, and looked up happily.

'*Je n'aime pas!*' said Graham, in an accent that had little hint of French in it, nor even a trace of his characteristic good nature. He was presumably anxious about our conversation to come. Yvonne picked at her food silently, emptied her glass, filled her ashtray.

Back at Graham's flat, adequately lubricated, the three of us sat down for a little discussion.

'Well, Rick, what do you think?' asked Graham.

It was hard to know quite what to say. The letters were interesting enough: I don't suppose they should be called love letters, but they were certainly loving letters, and the better for it. When animated by youthful lust his prose had suffered dreadfully.

'I'd love to buy them,' I said, 'they're extremely interesting!'

'Can this be done in confidence?' Yvonne asked uneasily. She was in a difficult position; Graham was keen to make the sale and was going to 'give' her the proceeds.

'It will certainly be in confidence today,' I replied, 'you can rely on that. But who knows what will happen tomorrow? I can promise to sell them to a discreet private collector. I can think of one or two. But then that person might die suddenly, and the next thing you know, the letters might be at Sotheby's.'

She looked alarmed, and glanced at Graham. She owned the letters, but she did not control their copyright, which was very much Greene's. If the letters ended up in a library, and were not embargoed in some way, then scholars might make 'fair usage' in quoting the contents.

'The fact is, Yvonne, you can't control material once it is out of your hands.'

'Never mind that,' Graham said, taking her hand, 'Rick will take care of it.'

It was a complex moment, and it had clearly been preceded by much discussion between them. I had the distinct impression that, though the letters were hers, the decision was his. I would not presume to say if this was usually the case between them, or whether this was how he usually treated his closest and dearest. It could not have been only about money: if Graham had wished to give Yvonne a sum equivalent to the value of the letters, he could certainly have afforded to do so.

I'm still unclear what he intended. A collector of books and paintings himself, he knew that things come and they go, are bought and sold and resold. A great many of his letters – including those to Catherine Walston – were already in libraries, and more would be in the future. Might it have been possible that he was engineering the very situation that Yvonne dreaded, opening up the possibility, however long term, that the letters might someday be in the public domain, filling in one of the many blanks in the Greene story? Yvonne was later to say of him that 'he left nothing to chance'.

I offered £15,000, which was a great deal more than Graham had anticipated, and he raised his eyebrows and smiled at Yvonne. A month later I sold them to a youthful, wealthy and healthy – and discreet – private collector, in whose keeping Greene and Cloetta might have supposed the letters would be safe.

In 1974, Greene appointed Professor Norman Sherry as his 'official' biographer, and gave him carte blanche to consult everyone and everything for the proposed book, and to publish his findings as he saw fit. Greene's line of thought was presumably that Professor Sherry was safe: he had previously published two books on Conrad (whom Greene revered) – *Conrad's Eastern World* and *Conrad's Western World* – in which he had followed doggedly in Conrad's many footsteps around the globe: visited the cities, the ports, the hotels, the very rooms in which Conrad had resided. In so doing, Professor Sherry had rarely evinced much interest in his subject's inner world: his attachments, dreams, fantasies, beliefs, aims or regrets. His Conrad books were literary travelogues.

I imagine Greene thinking: Perfect! Here is a potential biographer so lunatically assiduous that, having followed in my footsteps, there will be no later biographer following in his. Sherry would do the external ferreting, and leave the internals where they belonged, private. It was a promising if risky strategy, and by the time of the 1989 publication of Sherry's *The Life of Graham Greene: Volume I: 1904–1939*, it was clear that it had failed dismally. During the course of his researches, Professor Sherry had discovered the Inner World! He revelled in it.

A major catalyst for this transformation was Sherry's exposure to the remarkable series of letters written by Greene to his first wife, Vivien (née Dayrell-Browning), whom he met in Oxford in 1925. Their first contact was initiated by Vivien, then nineteen years old, a published poet of considerable acuity and strong views, who'd been working for Sir Basil Blackwell since she was fifteen.

Vivien had converted to Catholicism two years previously, and having read an article of Greene's that struck her as wrong-headed, she wrote to put him right. The offending passage in *The Oxford Outlook* read: 'We either go to church and worship the Virgin Mary or to a public house and snigger over stories and limericks; and this exaggerating of the sex instinct has had a bad effect on art ...'

There are good reasons to criticise this Madonna or whore Freudianism: why is it an 'exaggeration' of the sex instinct, rather than 'distortion'? And further, its 'bad effect' is surely on immature men, and thus on the art they may produce. (A relative of Greene's described him, at the time, as 'very under-developed'.) But Vivien's letter did not upbraid him for these reasons, but for his theological ignorance: one does not 'worship' the Virgin Mary, one 'venerates' her.

Well, that was provocative stuff; the young Greene wrote immediately to apologise. It was the first of what Sherry describes as an 'avalanche' – such an odd metaphor, similar in implication to his concurrent use of a 'bombardment' – of letters. Both images suggest the imminent, life-threatening dangers of love, which seems, well, a little odd. The young Greene's behaviour was compulsive to be sure, he sometimes wrote three letters a day, but the intention was hardly hostile and imminently destructive. Or was it?

He had ceded and conceded all the power to Miss Dayrell-Browning, and she was using it to a degree that pained him, and caused resentment: 'It must be rather fun collecting souls, Vivienne. Like postage stamps. Last addition to collection Undergraduate Versifier, a common kind . . . you will never be more than mildly interested in that blasted non-existent soul of mine . . . You can't sympathise, I suppose, any more than I can with the excitement of ants.'

The ensuing courtship was an agony of longing for the ardent young Greene, and his letters are ample testimony to this devotional frustration. Thus we have:

Wanted – by Me. Miss Dayrell
Alias Vivienne, Dear one, Darling, darling heart, marvellous wonderful, adorable one, Angel, Loveliest in the world, Sweetest heart, Dear only love for ever, sweet one, old thing, dear desire.

During the course of his long courtship – could one call it veneration? – of the upright and uptight Vivien, the perpetually upstanding Greene was first required to convert to Roman Catholicism (in 1926) before she would consent to marriage the next year. And this marriage, Vivien warned, must be celibate, as her lovelorn swain himself had suggested in desperation: a 'monastic' marriage: 'There'd be no domestic tying-down & you'd always keep your ideal of celibacy, & you could help me to keep the same ideal.'

Well, that didn't work, how could it? I once purchased from Blackwell's antiquarian department a series of Beatrix

Potter books that Greene had given to Vivien as gifts on Valentine's Day and other suitable occasions in the late 1920s. A copy of *Peter Rabbit* bears the besotted inscription: 'In love & adoration & worship & gratitude. To Puss from Wuff, Easter 1928.' This effusiveness is a neat example of the infantilising pathology of Edwardian whimsy, and circumlocution. Vivien was now properly Mrs Greene, celibacy by implication a thing of the past.

Norman Sherry read Greene's letters to Vivien avidly: what great material! How Inner can you get! In the first volume of his biography he quoted from them extensively. Greene read the draft of the book with chagrin, and asked his hyperactive Professor – whom he had begun to regard as his 'Inquisitor' – if it was necessary to cite quite so many letters, and at such length? Professor Sherry replied that indeed it was, and refused to make changes; that was their agreement, and Sherry was sticking to it. It was now up to him what would be made public, and how.

Greene felt exposed, and violated. Commentators routinely describe him as a 'secretive' man, fond of making double entries in diaries, one sanitised, and the other revealing information about his private life. This is often regarded as if it were a form of spycraft, as would be appropriate for a long-time member of MI6: the concealing of information, creating false trails, locations and plans. No wonder he wore that trench coat and trilby hat.

In its obituary of Norman Sherry, on 30 October 2016, the *Telegraph* observed that 'Greene hoped that Sherry would conduct an enquiry into the sources of literary creation rather than excavate his rampant sex life.' But surely this pedestrian explanation gets it wrong. When Greene told his biographer he could not bear someone 'crawling all over my life' (a curiously creepy phrase) he clearly meant more than his erotic life. A proud and private man, Greene was unwilling to be judged, not because of the extent of his sins but the inadequacy of his judges. It was not his sexual escapades that he was protecting, but his very nature. That would be judged on the day.

During one of my visits, Graham told me that he deeply regretted the whole biography business, which was to plague him not merely for the rest of his life (he died in 1991) but also the lives of many of his friends and relatives. Particularly Yvonne Cloetta. What must she have felt, reading in Sherry's first volume, those ardent youthful letters from her elderly lover to his wife? Not jealous, surely not, but envious perhaps? Of course the excesses of early passionate love are not replicated in later life, and may be replaced by something – as Greene was frequently to say to Yvonne – richer, deeper and more abiding. Less tempestuous, less fragile. I don't imagine this would have surprised or upset Yvonne Cloetta, but what would have given her pause – and she knew it was coming – was that in good time she would be the subject of prolonged analysis and dissection, etherised upon the page by Dr Sherry. That's how it would work: Volume 1 – Vivien; Volume 2 – Catherine Walston, the great passion of Greene's life; and then Volume 3 – Yvonne.

Norman Sherry had every bit as much fun with Catherine as he'd had with Vivien: Graham's letters to her are in the collection of Georgetown University Library, and he had carte blanche to quote from them. She is the dominating presence of *Volume 2: 1939–1955*. The first chapter to deal with their long, passionate affair is entitled 'Love as a Fever', and a later one 'Wildly, Crazily, Hopelessly'.

The relationship began, at Catherine's instigation, sometime in 1946. It was a difficult period for Greene, who was deeply depressed, and convinced that his best work was behind him. Separated from Vivien, he was now living in London with Dorothy Glover (who illustrated several of his children's books) and seeing other women, and not a few prostitutes, as well. (The *Telegraph* later announced breathlessly that at one period – it didn't stipulate which – Greene was having sex 'with five women at the same time', a phrase that suggests an unusual combination of libidinal power and social gregariousness.)

His feelings towards Catherine were expressed in a variety of forms. Obsessional in love, as always, and wounded that she would not leave her husband Harry to marry him, Greene wrote myriad letters, yearning and sometimes salacious, and of course *The End of the Affair* (1951), a barely disguised account of their relations. The following poem – published only after Catherine's death – reveals his heightened inward state:

> *I can believe only in love that strikes suddenly*
> *Out of a clear sky;*
> *I do not believe in the slow germination of friendship*
> *or one that asks 'why?'*
> *Because our love came savagely, suddenly,*
> *like an act of war,*
> *I cannot conceive a love that rises gently*
> *and subsides without a scar.*

I am trying, however fruitless and indeed fatuous the exercise, to read Sherry's account of this as if I were Yvonne Cloetta. What must she have felt, whose relations with Greene were of exactly the sort that are here brushed aside?

Though she would not have known it at the time of the publication of *Volume 2* (1994), her letters from Greene were no longer in private hands. After ten years, the owner of the Greene–Cloetta correspondence declared himself bored with the letters, having originally had the curious idea that he might publish them as a book (for which he would never have been given permission). Soon enough, the letters were not at Sotheby's, but in Georgetown University Library, the appropriate home, because Georgetown had extensive Greene holdings. It was not very long before the Cloetta letters were voraciously consulted by Norman Sherry, who had apparently been given sole access to the extensive Greene material that was held at Georgetown.

Volume 3 – Yvonne was still to come. What may have been alarming to her was not that Graham's letters reflected a 'lesser' intensity of love, but that they would be refracted through the consciousness of Professor Sherry. When she learnt that the letters were now at Georgetown, Yvonne wrote to me furiously, saying that I had promised that they would never come on the market. I replied that I had done no such thing, as no such promise could have been realistic. I reminded her of the details of our transaction, but she was neither convinced nor impressed. It had been foolish of me not to have written a letter at the time, to confirm the discussions we'd had in Antibes.

Greene died in Vevey on 3 April 1991, at the age of eighty-six. The *Guardian* correspondent reported the funeral as 'an affair as happily complaisant, in his sense of the word, as it was comradely and loving'. Amongst the intimate, the great and the good, was the crucial figure of Father Leopoldo Duran, who gave the sermon, and reported that Greene had asked for and received the last rites: 'I told him most directly, "Graham, God is waiting for you just now – pray for us where you will be for ever in God's blessing. I now give the last absolution." This I did. He passed away in the most peaceful manner. Without a gesture, he fell asleep. My faith tells me that he is now with God or on the way there.'

Vivien Greene attended the funeral, as did her children, and of course Yvonne Cloetta, who had a residence in Switzerland. Also present was Norman Sherry, though I am unclear whether by invitation or mere inclination. Yvonne Cloetta later told me, with a shiver, that at the graveside Sherry had insinuated himself next to her, to remind her that they 'must talk'. They didn't. The ramifications were several, and rather unpleasant.

If Yvonne was going to shun Norman, he still had access to the letters, and his account of them in *Volume 3* (2004) is ungenerous: 'His letters to Yvonne ... are sometimes dull, reflecting the tired love of an older man, listing what was on his midday plate ...' Indeed, the letters to Yvonne were not highly charged, as why should they be? She was the love of his later years, and though he was loving towards and with her, these letters were fond and newsy, full of descriptions of travels, places and people, of the work he was doing and contemplated. Might Yvonne have felt that these letters, compared to those to Vivien and then Catherine, were weak soup?

They were, according to Sherry: 'I felt she was out to prove to herself (and to the world) that Graham loved her, Yvonne, better than any previous lover. As my book proceeds, we'll be in a better position to judge whether Yvonne's view was justified. Love she felt for Greene. Absolutely. Was she taking herself in? I suppose to a degree this was so. Lying to oneself is not entirely unknown in humans.'

This is both unkind and emotionally semi-illiterate, and it was not in Yvonne Cloetta's nature to leave it unanswered; it was hardly up to Norman Sherry to curate the narrative of her relations with Greene.

I only understood what was happening in Yvonne's mind, as we sat there in the sunlight negotiating the sale of Graham's letters to her, when I read her book *In Search of a Beginning: My Life with Graham Greene*, which was published in 2004, explicitly timed to coincide with Sherry's third volume.

Her Foreword begins:

On 17 May 1989, as he handed me a copy of the first volume of Norman Sherry's biography, Graham said with a sad and gloomy expression, 'Poor you, I am afraid the day will come when you have to face some biographers. If I may give you any advice, this is what I would suggest: either you refuse to speak to them altogether – it's your right – or you agree to talk to them. If so, do tell the truth, but don't take a middle course.'

Her following reflection on this is revealing:

After his death ... My initial reaction was, of course, to say nothing and, selfishly, to keep all the many memories ... to myself. But the storm of hostility unleashed against him during the summer of

1994 . . .' [the year of Sherry's final volume, together with a hostile biography by an American academic named Michael Sheldon] *'. . . triggered such feelings of revulsion in me that I could no longer bear to maintain my silence, and so I have departed from what had always been our watchword in common: absolute discretion.*

This sentiment is reiterated several times: 'My whole life with Graham was one long secret. I learnt to keep my mouth shut.'

I suppose most readers would say, 'Good for you!' But from where I was sitting, it sounded doubly disingenuous: first, because Graham had hardly acted with 'absolute discretion' when he ceded to Norman Sherry the right to quote from his writings without consultation, and second, because Yvonne herself had sold her letters from him, thereby relinquishing control over their contents.

But she could at least tell her own story in her own words, and in those of her lover, whose most endearing and passionate letters to her are unrepresented in Sherry's text. She was not the compulsive first love of Greene's life, nor the tempestuous second, but as the third woman she had more time with Greene, and it was, by her account and often by his, happier and more satisfying (in every sense) than his previous fraught encounters with Vivien and Catherine, both of whom at one time or another had demanded an entirely celibate relationship, if only to have a bit of a rest from both man and God.

Let's give Yvonne – and indeed Graham – her own words. Her story is presented in a series of carefully honed conversations with Marie-Francoise Alain, whose role was to ask the prescribed questions. First, there was the necessary query about sex: 'We had an overwhelming need for one another ... I believe I provided him with moments of peace, passing ones, at least, through that total and mutual gift of oneself which is called, quite appropriately, "*la petit mort*" ...'

But second, there was more than sex, and better: at the end of his life, Greene confessed, 'I now realise that love – real, true love – between two human beings only reveals itself once it's no longer a question of sex.' Vivien and Catherine: eat your hearts out. She, Yvonne, had it all, and for longer and better. The third woman, perhaps, but demonstrably the best.

In the final volume of his biography, Norman Sherry provided an interesting footnote while writing about Greene in the late 1960s: 'In Singapore, I was hunted down by a French consul, who, knowing that I was Greene's biographer, wanted to shake the hand that shook the hand of the great one.' Sherry presumably obliged, and was so touched by this act of physiological alchemy, that he took it to heart and added it to his repertoire. Some thirty-five years later, I heard him speaking at the *London Review of Books* bookshop, which was right opposite my office. I got there early and claimed a front-row seat.

Professor Sherry began by describing himself modestly as a working-class boy who had had the most wonderful fortune to make an academic success of himself, and most remarkably to have been chosen as Graham Greene's 'official biographer'. He beamed at his audience beatifically. 'And this,' he said, raising his right arm and pointing his hand towards us, 'this is the hand that shook the hand of Graham Greene. And if you shake this hand, you are shaking his, through me! Shake it!'

He came forward, arm outstretched. Next to me his publicist buried her head in her hands, and I could feel the rest of the audience cowering and shrinking.

Sensing a sympathetic sap, Professor Sherry stopped in front of me. I took his hand, and shook it.

'Thank you,' I said.

By this time, though Norman Sherry's liabilities both as a man and a writer were writ clear over 2,200 pages, I still felt grateful to him. He had given half his life and a goodly portion of his sanity to his project, and though it is easy to patronise the final result, it is, as Greene had originally both conceived and misconceived, unsurpassable as a minute record of the writer's life. It is not a book to read entire, but if you want to know something about Greene at some period, or in some country or relationship, if you look at Sherry you will find out a lot.

It is, suppose I might say alas, but I will not, the biography of record, and we should be grateful for it.

5

Flagrant Fowles

In 2010 I received a fascinating catalogue, issued jointly by
Charles Cox and Maggs Brothers, which offered 'books from
the library of John Fowles'. Most significantly, it included the
author's heavily corrected copies of *The Aristos*, *The Magus*,
and *The French Lieutenant's Woman*, though they had already
been purchased, alas but rightly, by the University of Texas,
which holds the Fowles archive.

His library, or at least that twentieth-century remnant of it
detailed in the catalogue, gave an interesting window into his
inner life, though it is hard to say how many of the volumes
he purchased himself. Many were gifts, others sent to him by
publicists or publishers, perhaps hoping for a puff. The range
of the books was surprisingly random. Though there were
runs of titles by Julian Barnes, Ian McEwan, and Ted Hughes,
and smatterings by their contemporaries, Fowles' real enthu-
siasms were for earlier modern writers. He was a great admirer,
for instance, of John Collier, and had a run of editions of
Alain-Fournier's *Le Grand Meaulnes*, one of his favourite
books, and a clear influence on both *The Magus* (the only

book I have ever thrown out of a window) and *The Ebony Tower*.

Surprisingly few books were inscribed to him by other writers: none from Golding, whom he knew and admired, a few from Adam Thorpe and Christopher Priest, both of whose early works he championed, and the odd one from Richard Adams, David Lodge, Rose Tremain, and a few others. He seems not to have had many literary friendships, which was presumably, if not the cause at least the effect of living in Dorset. (Golding was also out of the loop, in Cornwall, and his library was similar to Fowles' in this respect.)

Fowles was an assiduous annotator, almost always sardonically, many of the books containing dismissive marginalia. Helen Fielding's first novel is called 'almost unimaginably bad', while Kenneth Tynan's *Diaries* elicit the observation that 'knowing everyone means in the end you know no one'. I wonder if he felt the reverse might be true?

I was a little surprised to see, as item 385, a copy of Graham Greene's *Victorian Detective Fiction*, which contains 'a note to JF from bookseller Rick Gekoski, referring to a meeting with Francis Greene, Graham's son. A note by JF explains that he had been asked to provide an introduction to a proposed new edition of this book.' At £450 it was reasonably priced, though of course I didn't buy it.

In 1966, Greene had published this book in an edition of 500 copies, signed by himself, his girlfriend the illustrator Dorothy Clover, and the bibliophile John Hayward. The title promised more than the book delivered: it was merely a catalogue of the books in his own collection. He'd assiduously amassed these many hundreds of first editions, most of them by book-hunting in country bookshops with his brother, who was also interested in detective fiction. To avoid bibliofratricide, they had agreed that Hugh would buy titles published after 1900, and Graham before then.

I first met John Fowles in November of 1989, at his beautiful if slightly gloomy Georgian Belmont House in Lyme Regis, when he was still, if not at the height, then in the middle phases of his reputation, which was largely built on the American overvaluation of his depth and uniqueness. An article in *The Spectator*, reviewing Elizabeth Warburton's biography of Fowles, quoted the following contemporary American assessment: 'The only novelist now writing in English whose works are likely to stand as literary classics ... who has the power, range, knowledge, and wisdom of a Tolstoy or James.'

The French Lieutenant's Woman stormed the gates of the Eng-Lit syllabus: how very exciting, how utterly post-modern! Can you believe it, there are three different endings! It made those slavering American academics quiver with delight as they set examination questions comparing Fowles with Tolstoy.

He carried himself commensurately with his reputation and his elegant house, a grandee, however introverted, whose every word and gesture seemed designed to show that he was smarter than you. It didn't bother me if, or that, he was. It was hardly like meeting Samuel Beckett, was it? I disliked most of his work, save that hauntingly creepy first novel, *The Collector*.

I was visiting at his invitation to buy a few books and manuscripts, particularly the original draft of his essay about Golding – entitled *'Golding' and Golding* – which had been printed in the Festschrift *William Golding: The Man and His Books. A Tribute on his 75th Birthday* (1986), which was edited by John Carey. I had rather a sore spot about that book, because when he was choosing the contributors, Carey had written to ask if I might consider doing an essay. Craig Raine had told him that I knew Golding, and Carey was at that point desperate for a contribution from someone who had a social relationship with his subject. Would I consider joining the party?

'Thank you, but no,' I said, 'I've only met Golding a few times, and could not call myself his friend. Indeed, I don't particularly like him, nor he, me.'

Carey wrote by return of post, offering lunch at Merton College to discuss the matter. I almost demurred – I should have done – but I was pleased to be able to meet Carey, whom I admired, and anyway Merton is my old college, and I like going back as something other than a nostalgic tourist. We made a date.

In the face of pressure and flattery I'm incapable of saying no, and before we'd even emptied our first glasses, I was on board, together with John Fowles, Ted Hughes and Seamus Heaney. This was fancy company, but I knew from the start that I was making a mistake: like many writers, I write best when I am excited by my subject, and can find the right voice. (Which was why my academic writing was so lifeless.) A few months later I submitted an essay entitled 'Golding's Beard', which told the story of my relations with him, and gave a measured assessment of his work (more interested in why things are than in how they are).

It didn't take Carey long to get back to me.

'I'm afraid I can't publish this,' he began. His reasons were fair, the same reasons I'd given in the first place: the essay

78

showed that I didn't know Golding very well and indeed that I didn't much like him. And, Carey admitted, he'd found someone who knew Golding better, and who both liked and admired him. I felt sore about this for a time, but Carey was right in every respect: it wasn't a very good essay, and it was inappropriate in the context of a Festschrift.

On my first visit to Fowles, I bought his manuscript essay about Golding for £500 (the same price I was later to pay Ted Hughes for his). Though he had no desire to sell any further manuscript material – his archive was at the University of Texas – I bought, for £1,144, a number of proof copies of his novels, and some inscribed books and proofs by other writers. I didn't really want most of them, but my foot, being in the door, had a desire to return.

What Fowles most wanted, though, was to get rid of the multiple copies of translations of his many works. 'I don't want these, or need them,' he said. 'I don't even know what language most of them are in, and they take up all this space ...' He waved at shelf after shelf of obscure paperback editions, on many of which the only decipherable words were 'John Fowles'.

'Are these wretched things of any value? They drive my wife mad!'

'If you mean scholarly value, yes, they might be useful to a bibliographer, or a Bulgarian enthusiast for your novels ... But if you mean financial value, then the answer is no.'

He looked a trifle disappointed. All that shelf space wasted, Elizabeth Fowles still furious every time she looked at the useless editions.

'I'll tell you what, though,' I continued, 'if you'd like, put them in boxes, and next time I come I can collect them and

79

donate them on your behalf to the University of Texas. They collect translations when they hold significant archival material by an author.'

Sometime later that year, I approached Graham Greene to inquire whether he might have something, a short story perhaps, for my Sixth Chamber Press. He didn't, alas, but compounded my disappointment by offering something totally unsuitable, a 'second edition' of the *Victorian Detective Fiction* book of 1966, which was in itself of little interest, being a motley assemblage of obscure titles, with few high spots: none of the rare Sherlock Holmes material was present, nor were the best Wilkie Collins titles. The book sold out because Graham had signed it, not because there were 500 fanatics yearning to know more about the subject.

Having no room to shelve the books after he decided to live in Antibes, Graham gifted them to his son Francis, who (at the suggestion of his father) was interested in republishing the catalogue under my Sixth Chamber Press imprint, incorporating his copious emendations, corrections, and additions. A scholarly, rather unworldly man, Francis felt that the new material was substantial enough to warrant a new edition. I disagreed, but fond feeling for Graham Greene himself made me wonder whether there wasn't some way to make it work, perhaps if I could get someone of note to write the introduction, and sign all of the copies. Greene himself wasn't interested – a sure sign of how unappealing the project was – nor was John le Carré. My third choice was John Fowles, who had the added advantage of living within a few miles of Francis Greene's house near Axminster. On 21 June, John, Elizabeth and I were invited to lunch with Francis and his wife to discuss the project.

Over the simple meal, in a foolish and provocative response to Mrs Greene's dewy enthusiasm for living in the midst of nature, I launched a mildly ironised attack on Wordsworth, and the folly of supposing one is improved by exposure to the natural world. Had he ever noticed how rough, dangerous and unforgiving nature can be? Give me art and cities anytime, I said, rather than the numbing effects of too many fields, streams, and drooling rustics. I most enjoy an exposure to nature when protected by a pane of glass: in a car driving through the Lake District perhaps, a train in Italy, or a room in a grand hotel overlooking a lake.

I was teasing, of course, but in the context it was inappropriate, and rude. This wasn't a dinner party in London literary society, and my hostess was rightly miffed. It was also an unpromising line of thought if you are trying to get John Fowles, an ardent student of the natural world, to do something for you. After lunch we repaired to the library, and John leafed through a few volumes of the Victorian fiction collection with scant interest. 'I simply have nothing to say about it,' he said as soon as we left.

I was relieved not to have published the book, but the collection itself intrigued me as a dealer. Though there were no collectors with sufficient interest to purchase such a collection (which wasn't generally in very good condition), there are libraries that collect in this area, or more broadly in late nineteenth-century fiction. Once I told Francis about Fowles' refusal, and that I therefore could not publish the book, he decided to sell, and invited Sotheby's to value the collection.

He soon told me that they had suggested an estimate of £6,000, which he regarded as an undervaluation.

'I agree, it's worth more than that.'

'I suppose I'll have to keep it . . .' he said ruefully.

'How much do you think it's worth?'

'Eleven thousand pounds!'

I have no idea how he reached this figure, but he was an exact and exacting man, and something of an antiquarian. It was from him that I learnt that a person in the seventeenth century who reached the age of thirty had a longer life expectancy than they do today.

'Can that be right?' I asked.

'Of course it's right. I did the work myself!'

I soon sent him a cheque for £11,000 and returned in a van a few weeks later to pick up the books, having constructed a wall of IKEA shelving in my bedroom to house the collection. It sold some months later to an American university library. Like Graham and Francis before me, I was relieved to get rid of it.

Here I must admit to a shaming habit. When I am in a bookshop, I sometimes look myself up in indexes of recently published books. After all, buying rare books and selling archives from well-known literary people means (many such being diary-keepers and gossips) that thoughts will be thought, then noted, and sometimes transmitted in print.

I have this sad habit under a degree of control. I don't seek myself in the index to *Wisden*, the *Guide to the Churches of East Anglia*, or books on birdwatching. But when I see an autobiography or book of memoirs, a *Collected Letters*, or published diaries or journals by someone I know, I often have a little peep. So, when browsing in the *LRB* bookshop in 2006, I picked up the newly published *Journals of John Fowles, Volume Two*, and turned to the index. And there I was: 'Gekoski, Rick, 381, 401–3'.

The entries began a trifle unpromisingly, and got worse. 'A big, bearded man, and Jewish,' I reminded him of 'someone from the Hollywood cinema world', which would have been quite flattering if you didn't know his opinions about that milieu. My reviews were mixed: 'A certain amount of "big" talk, valuable stuff he has had through his hands ... Difficult to have contact with that world without a feeling of nausea ... I quite liked him as people from that world go ... fundamentally sympathetic with his salt and cynicism well dominant over his trader self.' OK, I thought, I can live with that. It was followed by a business-like account of our dealing on the day: the buying of the manuscript and a few books, and the problem of disposing of the translations.

The second diary entry, though, brought me to a standstill, which is saying something in the *LRB* bookshop, where everyone else is standing still. But I was not languidly inert, I was paralysed. The facts were there: the lunch party at Francis Greene's house and little spat about Wordsworth (which had clearly irked Fowles as well as offending Mrs Greene). But the incessant refrain was that Rick is 'too Jewish for English tastes', partly, I suppose, because of my views about nature. Presumably, he might have felt equally hostile to Dr Johnson, who didn't much like it either.

More of the same followed: 'Rick himself remains a typical East European Jew, well soaked in the USA. He was obviously angry with "Bill" (Golding) for having mocked him, but had made it up as any proper Jew would, bending to the way of the wind, or the business and money pressure.'

I later wrote a few words in *Tolkien's Gown* about the apparent parody of me in Golding's *The Paper Men*, only to learn many years later from Golding's biographer John Carey – what goes around, comes around – that the invasive, bearded American biographer Rick L Tucker in that book is not based on me. Golding had used the name 'Rick' in the earliest draft of the novel, before he met me. I am mildly ashamed to admit that I was a trifle disappointed.

The experience with Fowles' journal entries left me a little bruised and a lot puzzled. How was I to understand the entries in the journal? Surely John Fowles, like TS Eliot, would have denied that he was an unregenerate anti-Semite, and in some pedantic sense he might have been right. Fowles was not manifesting a gross and universal hostility. He was hardly a member of Hamas. He was writing in his journals, as frankly as he could, under no obligation to be nice or proper, even about himself. He was self-doubting, painfully honest about his impotence and the constant discord with Elizabeth, and given to frequent barbed comments about Jews. What is surprising is that he should have chosen to publish them.

Since that time, I have come to regard that experience with Fowles as of general interest, and to be less forgiving. If his account of me was bruising, that aimed at his lifetime publisher Tom Maschler, of Jonathan Cape, was frankly disgusting. After dinner with Maschler and the distinguished American publisher Roger Straus, Fowles' journal entry reads: 'Jews like Tom and Straus make it so desperately difficult ... not to be anti-Semitic.' It's hard to parse the implications of 'make it so desperately difficult', as if it suggested some inward struggle and a desire not to succumb, but what really comes through is that such an experience made it easy for him, even necessary, to be anti-Semitic. He was sufficiently moved by the depth of evoked feeling to record this little poem:

Two Jewish Publishers
Deals, deals, endless great names, called all
By the first, of course, as in infant school;
They knew them well, these millionaire crows,
These jackal masters – though of what they wrote,
Of who they were at heart . . .
Nix, Literature, schmiterature, don't give us that.
We are back to the real, my friends:
Hawked carpets on the beach at Haifa.
Dollars, dollars, feel the pile, all is money.
If it were not a holocaust, it might be funny.

The next day, in self-praise and justification, Fowles wrote: 'My malicious and anti-Semitic contribution to the other evening. They asked for it.' The lines provoke a shiver of horror, and loathing: Those filthy Jews! Vulgar, money-grub-bing parasites! They got what they deserved!

Fowles' *Journals* were published in two volumes, in 2003 and 2006, the first of them two years before he died. Though friends and editors begged him to tone them down, to put it mildly, he resisted the advice: this is what his inward life was like. There are novelists, Fowles felt, who have 'a profound love-affair with the complexities of their own mind'. But why publish the results of this 'love-affair', when it was obviously unrequited? Fowles may have been entranced by the workings of his mind, but his mind was intent on betraying him. Rarely has a writer been such a sap for unmediated authenticity, whatever the revelations may have entailed: 'The truth about any artist, however terrible, is better than silence.' Counter-examples rush to mind; the overwhelming question being: why?

Hence the *Journals*, in which he felt it unnecessary to raise the portcullis between thinking and saying. That's what the form offers, after all. God knows why he was so pig-headed as to resist a degree of self-censoring, except as evidence for, and in praise of, his own forthrightness. They are his last (ill) will and testament. The entries are frequently excoriating about a serious proportion of the people he met, and (how crazy is this?) the publisher of the book itself. Maschler published most of Fowles' major works, and counted him a lifelong friend. After reading the journals, Maschler never spoke to him again, and did not attend his funeral in 2005.

As I, an American ex-pat who arrived in England in 1966, slowly learnt the unspoken codes and evasions, I began to understand that things that seemed innocent, or more strictly didn't seem anything at all, might be, in their gently inflected English manner, toxic. When I once went to stay with William Golding in Cornwall, while working on the bibliography of his work, Bill picked me up at the railway station in his old Jaguar. I admired it as we drove home.

'I'd love a new one,' he said, 'but I can't afford it.' It was the first of a number of his comments about being short of money. Once I saw his house and extensive gardens, and reflected about the lifetime royalties on *Lord of the Flies*, I rather doubted he was. After dinner and a lot of drink, I encouraged him to buy a new Jag.

'That's very well for you to say,' he responded, 'you're a rich man!'

I'm not. I later mentioned the incident to a friend who knew him well, and said I'd bet there are mentions of me in Golding's voluminous and fortunately unpublished diaries that contain mention of the J-word tonally similar to those in Fowles' *Journals*.

He said nothing.

Like Tom Maschler, having read the *Journals*, I was disgusted by the very thought of Fowles. But not long after his death, my office was approached by his literary agents Anthony Sheil Associates, acting for his widow Sarah, asking if we could arrange the sale of the rump of his archive to the University of Texas, which already had the bulk of the papers. I asked my colleague Peter Grogan to handle it, which he did with considerable dispatch, and patience.

The second Mrs Fowles, much younger than her husband, and unsophisticated in the world of libraries and archives, worried over the details: what was to be included and what was not? ... Who got to choose? ... Could some things be embargoed or held back for later transmission? A host of reasonable questions, pursued at considerable length. This is the real nitty-gritty of archive negotiations and delineations, and some of it also included questions about the *Journals*, which were originally going to be held back in Mrs Fowles' possession, but which Texas suggested be sent immediately, archivally preserved and then embargoed for a stipulated period of twenty years or until her death. Copies would of course be made for her records.

It was done, finally, and Peter went to Lyme Regis for a couple of days to sort out and package the relevant material, as now defined. Sometime later Belmont House was sold. Fowles wished it to become a writer's centre and retreat, a generous thought but something of a fantasy, as costs would have been prohibitive, and administrative structures and planning permission unwieldy. Instead, the house was sold to The Landmark Trust, which embarked on very substantial and expensive renovations, 'after eight years of detailed research, and two resolute years on site', before it opened for visitors' bookings in 2015.

Belinda and I, together with three friends, stayed there for three nights in 2019. The interior had been substantially reconfigured, the gardens uncongenially redesigned, but the outlook over the bay was as fine as ever, the downhill walk into Lyme still a delight. I told my friends a little about my relations with 'John', if I may be forgiven the Jewish informality, and showed them where the study and library were originally situated.

On the morning that we left, one of our party said, 'You know what? It's a very unhappy house. It feels creepy, like people were unhappy there.'

It is, and they were.

6

A Gentleman, and a Publisher

Unlike many of my colleagues I never advertise. I think it's a waste of money: what one needs is not self-promotion, but other-promotion. So every now and again, if I get something in stock that is unusual and perhaps even newsworthy, I may try to get it into one of the papers. This isn't particularly difficult – newspapers are omnivores, incessantly in need of interesting copy. But I wonder if this works very well either. You get some free publicity, but not much money. Sometimes, you even lose some. Not only do articles extolling the excellence of your stock often fail to attract buyers, they can also locate antagonists.

On 4 December 1997, the journalist Jim McCue did a piece in his 'Bibliomane' column in *The Times*, mentioning a tranche of Philip Larkin letters I was offering for sale, which were written to his friend and editor, the late Charles Monteith, the former Chairman of Faber & Faber: 'A mass of Larkin material currently being offered for sale includes a letter to Charles Monteith of Faber's with a wicked parody of Ted Hughes.

The sky split apart in malice
Stars rattled like pans on a shelf
Crow shat on Buckingham Palace
God pissed Himself.
Gekoski of Bloomsbury is selling the collection for £28,000.'

Monteith was one of the great publishing figures of his time – editor of Hughes, Beckett, Heaney and William Golding – a man of considerable acuity and probity, with a wicked sense of humour and endless supply of anecdotes. I first met him in 1983, when we were both staying with Bill and Ann Golding in Cornwall, and we met regularly if not frequently thereafter. He retired from Faber in 1980 due to ill health, which was not so extreme as to prohibit our jolly bibulous lunches at The Ivy. When he died in 1995, the *Independent* listed his many achievements and distinctions: Fellow, All Souls College, Oxford 1948–88 (Emeritus), Sub-Warden 1967–69; called to the Bar, Gray's Inn 1949; Director, Faber & Faber 1954–74, Vice-Chairman 1974–76, Chairman 1977–80, Senior Editorial Consultant 1981–95; Director, Poetry Book Society 1966–81; Member, Literature Panel, Arts Council of Great Britain 1974–78; Member, Library Advisory Council for England 1979–8.

A great man, and a good one.

The Larkin letters and postcards were largely written to Charles at his home address in Maida Vale, and though short of literary content, were always pithy and iconoclastic, entirely characteristic of Larkin at his jauntiest. Even when he's miserable, he's droll: 'I have felt very irritable, frightened, angry, depressed etc., quite unlike my usual sunny self ...' The last letter ends with yet another complaint about his declining health: 'No one except me seems very worried.' (He was morbidly pleased when he turned out to be right.)

In addition to the Hughes parody, there is a lapidary verse for a Jubilee plaque near Faber's in Queen Square:

In times when nothing stood
But worsened, or grew strange,
There was one constant good:
She did not change.

Comments on fellow writers are frequent – on Robert Lowell: 'Famous poets bother me ... if you see him, say I am renowned for my standoffishness ...'; and later: 'Lowell here last week – gt. drinking session!'; William Golding winning the Nobel Prize: 'How splendid for you ... though Wm. G. isn't really a man I read ...'; and WH Auden: 'There must have been someone nicer than CK [Chester Kallman] for WHA to get stuck with. Or was he one of those chaps like that appalling friend of Maugham ... the human equivalent of Tulip or Queenie or whatever its name was? You met him; you must have formed an impression. And how does one reconcile Auden's puritanical punctuality with the unbelievable slobbishness he seems to have welcomed?'

There are occasional references, too, to his own published work. About the poem 'The Old Fools': 'Although I took great trouble over the poem, I didn't think it entirely succeeded. There's always so much more to say ...'; and about the tribute volume *Larkin at Sixty*, profusely thanking Monteith for his efforts: 'I keep taking the book out – the leather one – and gloating over it. It is some consolation on the brink of the grave.' He also liked the paperback original edition of *Required Writing*: 'I think it looks a very buyable/sellable book ... chaps will be whipping out fivers everywhere.'

I bought these and many other letters, together with some photographs, on 2 December 1992, and Charles signed a letter of provenance affirming that they were 'my property and not that of Faber & Faber', after which I sold them to a collector in Philadelphia. Five years later, I bought them back from a New York dealer, and enlisted McCue's help in trying to find a buyer.

At 10.00am on the day his *Times* piece came out, I received a call from one Toby Faber, grandson of Geoffrey Faber and at that time a senior employee of the publishers. He was most interested in these letters, he said boyishly. Could he come round to have a look?

'I'll put the coffee on,' I said, without thinking. Why would someone from Faber want to come, immediately, to look at the letters? Had I been less hasty, I should have said, 'So sorry, what a shame, they are at my house in the country ...' In the light of what happened, though, this wouldn't have avoided the trouble to come, it would merely have delayed it, though it might have given me time to reflect and to strategise.

A few minutes later Mr Faber was in my office, reading through the letters, drinking his coffee, and munching on a fresh croissant.

'Thank you so very much,' he said, brushing off a few crumbs, 'they are very interesting.' He shook my hand and took his leave.

At lunchtime a writ from the High Court was served to me in my office, restraining me from selling the letters, and asserting that they were the property of the publishers. (How this could be obtained so quickly is a mystery to me.)

I got on the phone to Mr Faber, to inquire why he didn't simply tell me we had a problem?

'We were afraid that you would sell the letters and that we could not recover them,' he said. 'We are anxious to preserve the integrity of our archive.' According to Mr Faber, as the letters were addressed to their employee, the firm rightly owned those with significant literary content, and their Chairman, Matthew Evans was determined that they be returned.

I maintained, as Monteith had confirmed, that they were personal letters, bearing on friendship and not business, almost all of them addressed to his home in Maida Vale and not the office of Faber & Faber.

'I'm sure this can be resolved without recourse to litigation,' I said. 'Might I make an appointment to come in to your office to speak with Mr Evans, to explain the situation?'

'Mr Evans has no desire to meet you. I am dealing with the matter, and we are anxious to recover our property. May I come to retrieve our letters?'

This was unusually aggressive – apparently he'd been a boxing Blue at Oxford – and presaged a lot of biffing and jabbing to come. If the grand Mr Evans and the pugnacious Mr Faber had behaved like, well, gentlemen, as publishers once were and now so frequently are not, I would have been conciliatory, though I would not have given the letters back.

Of course not – they were mine. But I might have considered handing some of them over (not back) at my cost.

But if Faber's initial action obtaining a writ and injunction was aggressive, their next move was tantamount to a declaration of war. Two days after Mr Faber's visit to my office, there was a piece on page 2 of *The Times* – the 'News' section – by the arts journalist Dalya Alberge, with the headline: 'PUBLISHERS HALT SALE OF LETTERS BY PHILIP LARKIN'.

The article began with a fair summary of the problem, but by paragraph three had veered into contentious territory. Alberge quotes the 'wicked' parody of Ted Hughes, and continues: 'If, as Faber believe, it is the published example, it is an important document and should never have left their Bloomsbury archive.'

It isn't clear what is meant here by 'the published example', but that's not the major, and alarming, problem. The apparent claim is that the letter was once part of the 'Bloomsbury archive', and that it was, therefore, taken from it. Hence the clear implication that Monteith had improperly 'removed' it. But it was written to Monteith at his home address, and was never in the 'Bloomsbury archive', which was then stored in the old tunnels of the Eisenhower Centre in Chenies Street, near Goodge Street Station.

The article goes on to quote Matthew Evans: 'We believe some of the correspondence being sold is the property of Faber & Faber. We went round to chambers this morning to get an injunction to restrain Dr Gekoski from selling them until further notice. What we don't know is exactly what's there.'

'Publisher sues dealer' is not a promising headline if you're the dealer, whatever the outcome, and Ms Alberge gave me the final word, for what it was worth. I gave a summary explanation: 'I bought the letters from Mr Monteith with his written assurance that he was the owner of the letters. I always do this. He was a former Chairman of Faber & Faber and a man of the highest integrity. I have now no reason to question his judgement. I have done nothing either illegal or immoral, and have the fullest confidence that the matter will be resolved satisfactorily.'

Rubbish! I had no such confidence, in the light of Faber's aggression and hostility, that the matter could be resolved quickly or in a friendly manner. As a last resort I rang Mr Faber once more, to complain of his high-handed treatment. He declined to comment, and reiterated his demand that the letters at issue be returned.

'May I get this straight?' I asked. 'Forgive me if I misunderstand: Charles Monteith, your former Chairman, one of the great editors of his time, who incidentally was also a barrister, was incapable of distinguishing what was his and what belonged to his employer? I had the distinct impression from Charles that he was instrumental in framing your practices about such matters ...'

There was no response.

'... so if I understand the situation, you are accusing him of stealing the letters?'

'Of course not,' said Mr Faber, limply.

'Tell me why that isn't implicit in what you are doing? And if you believe Charles abstracted or improperly maintained possession of the letters you are contesting, why would you adopt such an aggressive stance with me, who would not have known this, and have acted in a professional manner?'

The call ended there. I put the phone down, and lit a cigar.

'Son of a bitch!' I said in a very loud voice, as I put my feet up on my desk, and said it again. I turned to my colleague Peter Grogan, sitting at the desk next to mine, who was son-of-a-bitching away loudly and shaking his head.

'I'll tell you what,' I said, 'I'll bet that if these Larkin letters were with establishment English book dealers like Maggs Brothers or Bernard Quaritch, Faber wouldn't be behaving in such a contemptuous manner.'

Peter knew what I was driving at.

'Indeed!' he said.

It suggested a strategy, and from that point I followed it: play to the stereotype. If they wanted a fight, they would have one. They might suppose me clever, self-satisfied and disputatious, rich and aggressive, as the clichés demand, but to these putative qualities I would add 'relentless'.

At the suggestion of my friend the lawyer and book collector Mark Everett, I soon employed his firm of Clifford Chance, as big, fancy and expensive a collection of international lawyers as London has to offer. My representative was one Michael Smyth, a literate and canny chap, who on first being told the facts of the case, was astonished at the imperious treatment I was receiving. He felt so strongly about this that he offered the lowest fee structure that he had available, which he acknowledged was still higher than most other firms. He was anxious to know my financial position.

'I cannot begin to afford to let this go on too long,' I said, 'unless you think it extremely likely that we will win, and recover costs ...'

He made the usual lawyerly noises, assurances followed by qualifications.

'Well, let's have a go,' I said. 'If they think I'm rich as well as stubborn, they might back off.' He promised to give me the meter readings as the clock ticked and bills mounted.

Months of litigation were to follow, in which I broke two cardinal precepts. First, never engage in a lawsuit with someone (much) richer than you are. Second, if you are foolish enough to do so, make sure the figures add up. Because within a month I had spent as much in lawyer's fees as the cost of the letters that Faber wanted returned.

I explained the situation and my strategy to a worldly and rich friend, himself no stranger to the judicial system. What advice might he have?

'You're an idiot! Give them back the letters. You're letting your ego get in the way.'

Fair comment. I was. That's what egos are for.

A few weeks after his visit to my office, Mr Faber requested a second meeting, in order that he and his colleague, the Faber Director John Bodley, who had a special interest in the Faber archive, might inspect the complete file of letters more carefully, in order to determine which ones Faber regarded as rightly theirs.

However furious I was, there was no sense in denying this request, and one evening the next week they came at my invitation to my residence in Primrose Hill 'for a drink' at

6.00pm. It was a lovely, recently renovated and decorated apartment in Chalcot Square, home to various illustrious and rich people: Robert Plant, Joan Bakewell, Nicholas Grimshaw. I would pretend to be one of them. Before Faber and Bodley arrived, I went round the corner to Bibendum wine merchants on Regent's Park Road to purchase a suitably impressive bottle of Puligny Montrachet – Bill Golding's favourite tipple. I put it in an ice bucket, took out three glasses, and rested them all on the mantelpiece below my beautiful Raoul Dufy oil portrait of Mme DeMarne, which had been greatly admired by Howard Hodgkin on a recent visit.

'You must never sell this you know . . .'

I'm a dealer. I sell things when I get the right price.

'. . . somebody like you will never be able to afford another picture as good as this!'

He was a clever man, and knew in an instant that I had limited means, and had lucked into possession of the painting, which I was now using as a prop to suggest just the opposite.

When the doorbell rang, Faber and John Bodley came in, and I hung up their coats. While Faber used the loo, Bodley whispered to me, 'I'm so sorry, I apologise for this.' The suggestion was that they were acting on instructions from Matthew Evans, and that he regretted it. (Amusingly, Evans once referred to Bodley as 'Faber's conscience', presumably a role he was unable to fulfil himself.)

I was beginning by this point to assemble an image of the Faber Chairman, who was well known to many of my publishing friends. He was clearly a man of great energies, a risk-taker and not a details person, a slavish companion of the great and the good. He loved the company of his writers, though it wasn't clear if he actually read them, and could be counted on to court anyone he regarded as a person of importance, never having understood – as so many of his writers did – that everyone is. He could be a bully. This combination of traits made him vulnerable.

Head of a publishing house with the best back list in the world, Matthew Evans was insufficiently competent to actually turn much of a profit. His nature and his views got in the way. Though in previous generations Faber had published beautiful and expensive signed, limited editions by Joyce, Eliot, Durrell and others, Evans thought such a market 'elitist', a ludicrous concept current at the time, and refused to issue any such. Thus Heaney and Hughes, pre-eminently, issued dozens of titles with a variety of small presses, depriving their primary publisher of very substantial income. It was only when (at Evans' suggestion) his fellow director Valerie Eliot agreed to a collaboration with Andrew Lloyd Webber, and then assigned a decent proportion of the profits from the musical *Cats* to Faber, that the company made some money.

A moment later I was drawing the cork from the fancy bottle of wine, standing under the expensive painting. On the mantelpiece were two Old Kingdom limestone canopic jars, one containing the lungs, the other the stomach of a long-deceased ancient Egyptian of some importance. A publisher perhaps. Having set the stage, I filled our glasses, and we sat down on the sofa and chairs, and made as little small talk as possible. I'd made some nibbles of smoked salmon on rye bread, with capers and a smear of wasabi by way of subliminal messaging. I put the file of letters out on the cocktail table and said I would leave them to it, and retreated to my bedroom. It was hardly an agreeable meeting, but I was enjoying it.

An hour-and-a-half later, after they had read, made notes and whispered to each other, they were finished. I returned and refilled our glasses.

'Thank you for this,' said Mr Faber. 'It's kind of you, you've been very fair, and it would be good if we could reach a quick settlement . . .'

'Wouldn't it! But if I may say a few things before we sit down formally to do so? First of all, I am on your side in this: I deal in writers' and publishers' archives, and place them in major institutions here and in America. I believe in maintaining the integrity of an archive whenever possible . . .'

They sat quietly, sensing a but. There were several.

'. . . but can I assure you: you have picked the wrong issue. And you have certainly picked the wrong man.'

They sat upright, still as ancient Egyptians.

'The facts are against you: for generations editors and directors at Faber threw away letters and galleys, and I have testimony from former employees to confirm this. It has long been the case that some Faber employees have sold material – letters, corrected galleys, and other material from Faber writers – at auction and in the rare book market. During discovery, we shall be subpoenaing all your present and past living editorial staff to determine the scale of this. The fact is that Faber have only recently, in the person of your Chairman, decided to establish a notion of "the integrity of the archive". We shall be asking for you to produce any boardroom minutes, memoranda or instructions, that set out rules for what is to be done with regard to this undefined, and I gather previously unrecorded concept, of archival "integrity".'

I had in my desk drawer a copy of a letter that I could supply to back up my claims, but not yet. It was written to me in November of 1989 by the senior Faber figure Peter du Sautoy, suggesting that he might sell me some of his letters from Eliot, Britten, Golding and Larkin. He wrote at the time: 'My trouble is that I am a bit reluctant to sell owing to the personal friendships involved. But I suppose that I may be forced to, or my wife might find it necessary. We shall be glad to keep you in mind.'

Good scrupulous reasoning, and no mention of the archive. I had many other such, from other Faber employees from whom I had purchased material.

Mr Faber rose to his feet, and Mr Bodley followed. Both of them now confirmed that I was an innocent party in the matter, and had acted entirely properly and openly in granting them access to the material: the clear implication being that Monteith, a man of great probity, had acted improperly in selling the material to me. Not to put too fine a point on it: stolen it. But Charles, of course, was one of the people at Faber – perhaps the person – who had worked at defining the distinction between business letters and personal ones. This seemed to cut no ice with Matthew Evans, who clearly did not mind if Charles was publicly, and posthumously, implicitly branded a thief.

'I'm sure we have taken enough of your time,' said Mr Faber. 'Thank you for your forthrightness, and your hospitality. We will be in touch regarding the next step.'

When they'd left, I put their glasses and plates in the dishwasher, skimmed the wasabi off the canapes, and ate them for supper with the remains of the excellent wine. It had been a most satisfactory meeting. It would be hard for them to recover momentum.

A week passed, and I had no word from them. I let a few more days go by, no need to seem anxious, then wrote Mr Faber an email asking where we now stood? There was no reply. I rang his office, and left a message. No reply. I tried the same with Mr Bodley, and just for the fun of it, Mr Evans. Nothing. Perhaps they'd all gone off on a retreat to do some corporate bonding.

After a few more days, my lawyer had a letter from theirs, indicating that henceforth all communication would be through the legal channels. Obviously Mr Faber and Mr Bodley had had a bollocking on their return, and were lucky not to find their viscera at the bottom of a jar. Perhaps Mr Evans was unimpressed by their account of my sweet reasonableness, that's not what you send your surrogates to elicit. The new strategy was clear: bombard my lawyers with communications of one unnecessary kind or another, demanding replies in detail. Money. They had a lot more of it than I, surely? Keep the costs mounting, and see if I would cave in.

Michael Smyth wrote a scathing letter outlining the points I had made at my meeting with Faber and Bodley, requesting answers to them. It was in this period that Evans, clearly impatient, made a critical mistake. Unable to find any internal evidence about Faber's formal criterion for material to enter the archive, he made one up. A letter arrived in which the Faber Chairman, after the expected sorts of waffle, gave a crisp definition of what he considered his employees' archival obligations: *all material written from a writer to his editor is the property of the publishing house.* Matthew Evans was inventing a new policy to apply retrospectively, not enforcing an old one. This was remarkably silly, contrary to practice, dangerous, stupid, tyrannical. No letter from a writer to his editor, however personal, could thus be regarded as private, even when sent to his home. No writer or editor could agree to such constrained relations.

I couldn't have hoped for more: on 9 January, I began a campaign to expose this nonsense as widely as possible. I began by issuing a formal, detailed complaint – copying in Faber – to The Antiquarian Booksellers Association, for the case would have implications for the trade in manuscripts and archives. It was at this point that I learnt that there was history to Evans' harassment: a few years before, the widow of the late Bernard Wolpe, a distinguished designer at Faber, sent some of her husband's material to auction at Bloomsbury Book Auctions, including some galley proofs that Wolpe had rescued from a wastepaper basket in the Faber offices. Frank Herrmann of Bloomsbury Book Auctions, who had worked at Faber for many years, says they often threw away such material – galleys, proofs, letters, etc. – in large quantities. According to Herrmann, Evans immediately threatened Bloomsbury Book Auctions with legal action, unless they withdrew the Wolpe material from sale, and also threatened the widow Wolpe with the withdrawal of her pension from the firm unless she returned the material. The elderly Mrs Wolpe, most distressed and alarmed, capitulated.

It was disgusting, and it strengthened my resolve, and perhaps my initial diagnosis. The high-handedness with which Matthew Evans had been treating me might or might not have been anti-Semitic, it might just have been because he was a bully. People who knew him said they could find no trace of such prejudice in his character, and he had many Jewish friends (as if that rendered him spotless). But this new instance of bloody-minded harassment also victimised Jews: the Wolpes and Frank Herrmann. I still hesitated to think of this as confirmation of my suspicion: there are a lot of Jews in publishing, though not that many at Faber & Faber. Perhaps they were shooed away by TS Eliot?

There had been a creeping change in the culture at Faber & Faber, with a markedly diminished capacity to attract high-quality editors, commission important new writers, or even keep some of their old ones. Aside from *Cats*, they were doing pretty badly. And their decline – I do not think you could call it anything else – correlates, I think, to the end of a period in English publishing and English culture. Aside from the estimable John Bodley, I cannot think of anyone that I knew there who was a patch on Charles Monteith.

I soon consulted my friend Tom Rosenthal, a book collector and the distinguished owner and Managing Director of André Deutsch Publishers, previously Chairman of both Heinemann and Secker & Warburg. I told him of my letter to the Antiquarian Booksellers Association, but he laughed.

'Matthew won't give a damn about that! No, what you need to do is put him on the defensive, and humiliate him publicly. I will do an article for the *Sunday Telegraph*, but what would be best is if you write formal letters of complaint to both the Publishers Association and the Society of Authors. Both of them will recognise nonsense when they hear it, and follow it up, and it will piss Matthew off.' He added that Evans could be a bully, and worked assiduously at his image: 'he's desperate for a gong'.

The letters were duly sent (cc to Faber & Faber) and elicited thoughtful alarm from both bodies, particularly with regard to the new definition of the epistolary relationship between a writer and his publisher.

Next I wrote to Bill Buford, then Literary Editor of the *New Yorker*, a man deeply rooted in English literary culture after his many years editing *Granta*. I'd met him several times socially, sufficient to write a letter detailing the problem, suggesting that I write a piece about Monteith and the ensuing shenanigans, entitled 'The Last of the Gentlemen Publishers'. I had a long phone call with Bill a few days later. He was distinctly interested, though he favoured a shift of emphasis from the late Monteith to the alleged change of culture at Faber & Faber. I made sure, through a friend, that Evans got word of this as well.

Some further time passed, some weeks, some more correspondence.

Faber made their case, indicating exactly which Larkin letters on which dates they regarded as their property.

I made my case, reiterating that I was not going to give them back.

Clifford Chance made their money.

I did not begrudge the rising costs, which would confirm to my antagonists that I was in it for the long haul. A High Court case can cost £100,000 – my bill at Clifford Chance was already well over £10,000, and the retail value of the letters now at issue was less than that – and even if I won, I was by no means guaranteed to recover costs. And there I was, carrying on. Never waver. Do not suggest a meeting or a negotiation.

The suggestion came from Mr Faber himself, over the phone.

'Don't you think this has gone on long enough? Would you come by my office, please, and let me know what it would take to reach a settlement?'

He repeated the question a few days later when, after a perfunctory handshake, I was seated in front of his desk, as if being interviewed for a junior position. He leant over benignly, years at the firm having given him an elderly mien.

'Tell me what you might suggest to get us over this.'

After a short and by no means cordial negotiation I achieved the result I wanted: reimbursement of my legal costs (something over £13,000) and payment, at cost, to me for the letters they claimed were properly theirs.

I would have liked him to send a letter to *The Times*, withdrawing the allegation of misconduct that had been made, and confirming that my behaviour had been professionally exemplary. Of course, I never expected he would: in a negotiation, you have to give the other side something to turn down, and to feel good about. He was a tough guy! I didn't care: the issue was unlikely, after all these months, to be in anyone's mind, and a statement from Faber would only reawaken the memory. By this time, I was making the mistake to suppose that Toby, having been booted into the role of attack dog, might be an OK chap after all. Perhaps I'd been naïve, unused to the tougher ways of corporate life?

The generosity of this forgiving impulse was shattered in a moment.

'I still believe,' he said, rising from his desk with a facial expression that would have been wolfish had he a wolf in him, 'that you knew all along that it was a dodgy deal, and that's why you had Charles sign the letter.'

I hardly trusted myself to respond to this gratuitous low blow, gathered my coat, and left the room. I don't recall that we ever finalised the agreement formally, but the necessaries were soon done, though they left an abiding bad taste. It was over, I'd been headstrong, and I got a result. Risky, overly self-confident, flamboyant! Perhaps I was the Matthew Evans of book dealers?

★

After his early retirement as Managing Director of the firm, Toby Faber threw himself headlong into the blessed archive, which became the basis for his book *Faber & Faber: The Untold Story* (2019), which relies almost entirely on quoted material from Faber authors and editors, interspersed modestly with accounts of the firm's administration. Though many Larkin letters are printed, none of those that I returned to Faber were cited.

In the Honours List of 2000, Matthew Evans was made Baron Evans of Temple Guiting. The term 'Guiting' derives from the Anglo-Saxon 'gyte' and means a dangerous outpouring.

7

The Mystery of the Nine *Ulysses*

'HAPLESS BOOK DEALER LOSES NINE FIRST EDITIONS
OF JAMES JOYCE'S MASTERPIECE!'

*Published in Paris in 1922, by the young American Sylvia Beach,
James Joyce's* Ulysses *was issued in an edition of 1,000 copies.
The nine priceless copies were lost after they had been entrusted to
the London book dealer Gekoski, to sell on behalf of the University
of Texas.*

I drafted it myself, this headline, scribbled it into my head,
wrote and rewrote it, scalded by loss and humiliation, as the
luggage carousel at New York's LaGuardia Airport emptied,
and the last passenger removed the final bag.

I stood gazing as anxiously and longingly at the opening as
a prospective father in a delivery room. The conveyor belt
stopped. No further bags appeared. The hall emptied. An
ominous silence established itself.

The term 'priceless' is for lazy dopes and headline writers.
I added it up again and again. I'm a dealer – I knew the prices

clearly enough: 2 copies of the edition of 100 signed by Joyce @ £30,000; 2 copies of the edition of 150 copies @ £15,000; 5 copies of the edition of 750 copies @ £8,000.

That made a total, more or less, of £132,000, or $225,000. I was insured, but the money wasn't the point. The books were lost, not merely to Texas, or to and by me, but to the world. There is a census of the extant copies of the issues of both 100 and 150; in the future, the lost copies, with their numbers, would be registered as 'lost by RA Gekoski'.

I knew it. I bloody knew it. It was all my fault, wasn't it? Was it?

Like all tragedies, it started well. Oedipus is perched on the Theban throne, happily married, prosperous, a bit smug. Soon he is tearing his eyes out and cursing the gods. That sort of thing. My own auspicious beginning involved a phone call early in 1994 from the redoubtable Tom Staley, then the Director of the Harry Ransom Center at the University of Texas, Austin, the greatest American depository of modern books and manuscripts. He'd been doing an inventory of their extensive holdings, and decided that they had many more copies of the first edition of Joyce's *Ulysses* (Paris, 1922) than they (or anyone) needed. Professor Staley fancied a bit of a clear out, and wondered if I might like to be of service?

'I've chosen nine of them, all in nice condition, and I wonder if you could sell them for us? Why don't you come over to discuss it, and if we agree terms – and we will! – you can take them home.'

'Works for me!' I said.

'When would you be able to come?'

'Well,' I said, 'any day at all, starting tomorrow.'

'I'm so grateful to you,' said Tom.

I was then a frequent visitor to the HRC (either Harry Ransom Center, after its founder, or Humanities Research Center, or both), sometimes for conferences, occasionally to give talks, at other times just for the fun of it. I'd grown very fond of Tom Staley, had frequent meals with him and his family; for we shared a passion not merely for books but for sport. He'd been a professional baseball player in his youth, and in his sixties was a keen tennis player, who often played in Seniors Tournaments. He had a dogged all-court game, scooted about assiduously, and hated to lose. On one of my visits he kindly included me in his weekly doubles, when his partner had to drop out.

Our opponents included WW (Walt) Rostow, Special Assistant for National Security Affairs under LBJ, and one of the most hated political figures of my generation. I was longing to ask him how American 'national security' had necessitated the death of tens of thousands of Vietnamese, and so many American boys, who would not have known the answer themselves. Sometimes I'm too nice. In his courtly incarnation, as long as he didn't have to move about much, Rostow played competent doubles for a man of 81. When he was at the baseline, I hit drop shots whenever I could. He never reached any of them, and after the first few glared as if he'd like to napalm me.

Staley's energies, which exhausted everybody except him, had grown the HRC from an oak tree into a veritable forest. Collections boomed and expanded, and the range of their holdings of authors' archives, Tom's major passion, rose exponentially. Under his leadership 'Texas' became the code word for omnivorous acquisition, and when said in an English accent had both contempt and fearful respect laced into it. Various British luminaries, like Poet Laureate Andrew Motion, objected in print to the potential loss of 'our literary heritage', as if literary heritages disappear when they move abroad. Two things seemed inevitable in this scenario: Death and Texas.

There was, as Staley admitted unsheepishly, some truth in this charge of literary hijacking. Under his leadership, Texas had acquired the archives of Julian Barnes, Tom Stoppard, David Hare, Penelope Lively, Doris Lessing, Barry Unsworth, and many other British writers. (And, since his retirement and replacement by Steve Enniss, a great many more, including Ian McEwan and Kazuo Ishiguro.) Staley saw no need to defend his appetite for such acquisitions: no one, as he often observed, could make an author sell their papers abroad. But he provided good reasons for doing so. Compared to the British Library, his major competitor for English literary archives, Texas could act more quickly, get the material cata-logued and preserved more efficiently, and pay more expedi-tiously. As well, often, as more.

This was not, as is frequently assumed, because they had gushing wells of money to fund such purchases. In fact, Texas have, on average, $2 million a year for acquisitions, which, while a nice amount, is very much less than, say, the British Library, or indeed several other leading American institutions. No, what Texas has is a great hotline, and a very considerable number of wealthy donors at the end of it. Thus, for instance, when they bought the Watergate papers for $5 million in 2003, there were so many keen benefactors in the queue that

Staley made a rule that no one was allowed to give more than $500,000. It didn't take long before the money was in the collection box. And the papers didn't even reveal the identity of 'Deep Throat'!

I arrived in Austin a seemly week after Tom's offer of the nine copies of *Ulysses*, went directly to his office, and found them laid out on his desk. Of course, I had handled each of the three issues of that text frequently, but I'd never seen so many at once. Hardly anyone has. I went a bit quiet, moved over to the table, and examined them in silence, one at a time. The fat 1/100s, the tall, elegant 1/150s, the trade editions of 750, all in a row in their ravishing blue paper covers. Tom was grinning to himself, fully aware of what a treat he was offering.

'Wow!' I said, or maybe it was 'Gosh!', something childishly inadequate, and perfectly framed. He'd chosen excellent copies of the books in their original wrappers, clearly with the aim of increasing their market value and saleability.

'What do you think?' he asked puckishly.

I said something childishly inadequate. Thought for a moment, and asked, 'What's the deal?'

'Let's get some lunch,' he said.

Over lunch we talked about (other) books, sport, various friends in the bookselling and literary worlds, and studiously avoided the matter at hand, until it became a matter of interest, pride really, to see which of us would crack first. Like some sort of funny sport.

We walked the few blocks back to Tom's office, which took some time, because he knew almost everyone along the way, and always stopped to inquire 'How are you?' His emphasis of this phrase was not (as usual) '*How* are you?' or 'How are *you?*' Tom said, 'How *are* you?' as if he were taking an existential census: 'How'd you come to be?' ...'What sort of being might that be?'

This rendered the usual answer 'Fine' more than insipid but illiterate, though the alternative 'Well, I've thought about this a lot; Murleau-Ponty says ...' is hardly appropriate, however great the temptation. Usually, I just responded to Tom with the same question, and the same emphasis (which takes some practice). He always answered 'Just fine,' as if the 'just' explained everything.

As he and his various acquaintances passed the time of day, I waited patiently, visions of Aegean blue books dancing in front of my eyes. When we got back to his office, he sat behind his desk.

'Well,' he said, 'I'm so happy we can do this. Here's what I suggest – I will get an appraisal of the books from Howard Woolmer ...' – an excellent American book dealer with wide experience handling Joyce material – '... and then if you can sell the books at his estimates, you can have 30 per cent.'

This made me hesitate.

'Well, Tom,' I said after a few moments of face puckering, 'I'm afraid I can't accept those terms ...'

'Why ever not?'

'I'd suggest that I take 20 per cent.'

He went silent, his brow furrowed, he scratched his head, and looked over at me curiously, as if about to inquire 'How are you?'

'Let me get this straight. I have offered you 30 per cent?'

'Yup.'

'And you are counter-offering 20 per cent?'

'Indeed.'

'Why would you do that?' he asked, incredulously.

I wanted to ask him the same question about the sale: How did you decide to sell off these important books? Is there a precedent for such a sale? What is the procedure? Of course, libraries sell books constantly, very often because they have been left them in various well-meaning people's wills. Librarians dread such bequests. Donald Eddy, formerly the Head of Cornell University Library, told me that he once had to make plans to assimilate thousands of law books which had been bequeathed to Cornell by an eminent lawyer. His proud widow wanted them kept in a special room, with the lawyer's name on it. Cornell had every one of the books already, and Don noted that it cost roughly $25 to enter a book into the library system, much less to create and maintain a room to house the worthless collection.

'I had to figure out a way to say no,' he said plaintively, 'but the widow was a trustee of the University ...'

Many of the major American libraries have yearly sales of thousands of extraneous books, and local dealers queue for hours before the sales open. Most of them are disappointed, because most of the books, like many of the dealers, are not very exciting. It's like a jumble sale, only the wares are more plentiful and less good.

But nine copies of *Ulysses*? Texas hadn't been bequeathed them in anyone's will, that's inconceivable – no, the plethora of examples was created in the early days of the growth of Texas's collections. From the mid-1950s, the Library Director Harry Ransom bought multiple collections and personal libraries from fabled collectors and writers, many of whom had substantial holdings of modern classics. Hence the duplicates, which had festered, like bedbugs: no one knew, quite, where they'd come from, nor why there were so many of them.

Ransom also bought in ones, if he could get enough of them in a single bite, as a whale may live on plankton if it swallows enough. His book dealer of choice was one Lew David Feldman, whose New York firm, the mock-Arabic House of El Dieff (LDF, get it?) rose from modest beginnings to become a leading dealership of the time, largely because of its association with Texas. Ransom bought manically, and Feldman executed his bids with ruthless delight. In the 1960s, the University of Texas spent $17 million, which had gushed from a desolate spread of land owned by the university, on new collections and manuscripts.

Soon enough, Feldman was sufficiently rich to allow the flexibility of deferred billing: by 1970, Texas owed him some $3 million (or some $20 million at today's rates, adjusted for inflation). This did not go down well, as might be expected, with other members of the rare book trade. Charles Hamilton's *Auction Madness* (1981) characterises Feldman thus:

> *The ability to bilk one's clients is a fine art ... To exceed for a lifetime without detection or exposure, the auction-buying crook must have the cunning of a polecat, the ethics of a gabon viper, and the acquisitive drive of a dung-beetle. All these feral qualities were uniquely fused in the late Lew David Feldman ...*

One time, early in the 1960s, Feldman got an instruction from Ransom to fly to London, where there was going to be a major auction of important modern first editions, manuscripts and associated material. Buy the entire sale! Feldman purchased a first-class ticket, hurried to Idlewild Airport the morning before the sale, and on arrival that evening ensconced himself grandly in a West End hotel, had a few drinks, and went wearily to bed.

His *New York Times* obituary (30 November 1976) mentioned what happened next:

> *In fact, he was probably the only man who bid on 56 successive items at Sotheby's London while dressed in pajamas, a robe and a raincoat. He had gotten up late and was so fearful that he would miss out on the bidding that he simply put on a raincoat and headed for the auction rooms.*

I love the 'probably' in that first sentence: had other dealers bid on fewer successive items in their pyjamas? Or more successive items, but properly attired?

Feldman sat in the front row, and from Item 1 onwards he raised his arm at half mast, and left it there through the sale. I suppose he must have shaken it between items, so it didn't get numb. At the end of the auction, he sent a telegram to Ransom, explaining that he had purchased all of the items except two, which had exceeded the estimate by ten times. He got a curt reply, 'I didn't send you to London to not buy the damn books!'

What might Ransom, or even Feldman, have thought of Staley's decision to sell off the excess copies of *Ulysses*? It's a nice question, but who cares? Things move on: Staley was minded to de-acquisition (terrible term) some of them, which seemed to me sensible, but then again it would.

Though Texas held (I think it was) twenty-seven copies of Joyce's masterpiece, there are some scholars who believe that, such was the amateurishness of the book's production, a strict collation might well reveal textual variants between copies, though who would care about these – save textual variant fetishists – is unclear. The Folger Shakespeare Library, in Washington, has eighty-two copies of Shakespeare's First Folio (1623) and they have no intention of letting a single one leave the premises. They are all demonstrably different! To the question: 'Who gives a damn if they are?' the answer is: 'We do!' Either this is not true of *Ulysses*, or the differences are insufficiently compelling to justify retaining cupboards full of them.

I looked once again, increasingly fondly, at the copies of the book in Tom's office.

'Why have I offered to do this at 20 per cent? Two reasons: first, the books are eminently saleable, and will look good in my catalogue. I don't have to take out my wallet to buy them, so 20 per cent is ample. And, second, I want you to have a smile on your face next time I come to your office ...'

'I always do,' said Tom. 'Thanks for that, I'll get someone to wrap each one safely, do you have something to put them in?'

'I brought a large empty suitcase, with hard covers.'

'Perfect!'

He picked up his phone to make the necessary arrange-ments with his packing department, and I went back to my hotel to rest, shower, and gloat. I fancied getting some good ol' Texas barbecue for supper, and asked several members of the HRC staff to suggest the best place.

'Y'all wanna come along?' I was surprised to hear myself asking. I'd been in Texas for two days and all of a sudden I'm a cowboy? I'm not usually seduced by regional accents, indeed I have lived in England for over fifty years and still sound distinctly American. What is it about the American South that makes its tones so adhesive? Think of George Bush, an East Coast preppie, now sounding like a Texas rancher. Or indeed Staley himself, brought up in Pittsburgh, now sufficiently linguistically assimilated to his new environment, almost as if he were a member of the Austin Kiwanis Club. He has to talk to a lot of very rich Texans, to get along with them, get them on board, and spend their money. Best to sound, well, plausible. They don't much like Yankees down there.

I disgraced myself at the barbecue joint as well. When asked at the counter – there was no waitress service, of course, this was authentic – how many beef ribs I wanted, I replied, 'Eight'. There were unrestrained hee-haws and gee-whizzes, and much slapping of knees.

'Eight, boy! You best start with two!'

I couldn't finish those. They make things big in Texas.

The next morning, I popped round to pick up the books, which fitted into my new suitcase as if it were constructed to house them. Within an hour, the taxi had taken me to Austin airport, with plenty of time to check in before my departure for New York LaGuardia, where my sister would be meeting me.

This might, I realised, be a little tricky, but the pleasant young woman at check-in for Southwestern Airlines looked a pushover for a touch of the old Anglo–American charm. I had form dealing with customs agents. I once arrived at JFK from London, my suitcase was opened and searched – remember when they did that? – and the formidable agent soon discovered a box of twenty-five Montecristo Cigars. She took it out gingerly, between two fingers, as if it might be contaminated.

She studied the label, which confirmed her doubts.

'We don' much like these folks,' she said, pointed to the 'Habana' label. It is still illegal to import Cuban cigars to America.

'Well,' I said, 'may I explain . . .?'

'Yeah? What?' she said, preparing to confiscate my treasures.

'Well, speaking frankly, it's a trifle humiliating, but I am addicted to these cigars. It's a medical condition. I smoke three a day, one after lunch, one after dinner, and one late in the evening. Without them I am a nervous wreck, and unable to function without psychiatric assistance. Here's my proposal: there are twenty-five cigars, and I am coming for eight days, so I am in dire organic need of twenty-four of them. Could you just take the extra one, and we could call it quits?'

She made no move to return the box to my opened suitcase.

'If you'd be kind enough to inform me,' I said, a trifle unctuously, 'in what manner I can throw myself upon your mercy . . .?'

She looked me in the eye, peered again at the Montecristos, and put them back into my case.

'Ah, ged oud'a heah!' she said, without so much as a smile, and I scuttled off as quickly as Groucho in need of a smoke.

Copies of *Ulysses* are no longer banned from the United States – that ended in 1933, after the legal case United States v One Book Entitled *Ulysses* – so getting them on the plane with me should have been a doddle. I had no intention of letting my goodies disappear into the hold, where they'd likely freeze to death, or get mislaid or mishandled. They were coming on board with me!

Informed that I intended to take the suitcase as carry-on luggage, the check-in agent took one look at it, observed that it would hardly fit in an overhead locker, and would have to be checked in.

'I'm afraid I need to take it on board. The contents are very fragile and valuable, and I can't risk them being damaged. If it won't fit overhead, may I buy a seat for it next to me? It won't be any trouble, and doesn't require lunch, or a sick bag . . .'

'What's in it?'

The answer 'nine rare books worth a quarter of a million dollars' was inadvisable.

'Family heirlooms,' I said, 'they're very precious to me. From my dear mother who has recently died.' My eyes welled up.

'Sir, I'm sure they'll be safe. What I can do is put special wrapping round the suitcase, labelled FRAGILE, and that will be sufficient to ensure its safety.'

Hah! What that would ensure, I thought, is that the baggage handlers would toss it about for a bit of fun, before throwing it like a shotput into the gaping maw of the hold. Even very slight damage to the delicate paper covers of the books could cause tens of thousands of dollars of damage.

'Ma'am,' I said, 'y'all been most kind, how's about we upgrade myself and my companion to First Class? There's plenty of room up there ...'

'I'm sorry, sir, that's impossible.'

'In that case, may I speak to the flight supervisor?'

'I am the flight supervisor,' she said.

The people queueing behind me, who had followed the initial exchanges with some interest and amusement, were getting impatient as I contemplated my options – catch another flight with a more sympathetic airline? Send the books by FedEx? Drive them all the way back to the East Coast? No, nope, never. They were insured in transit. They'd be fine ...

'OK, I give up,' I said to the increasingly hostile young woman. 'Take the bag.'

'Thank you, sir ... have a nice flight.'

I didn't, I worried and fidgeted, imagining my dear, very valuable books shivering just below me. It got a whole lot worse after we landed, as I waited in vain for my suitcase to come on to the luggage carousel. I knew it wouldn't. I knew it. And it didn't. Soon enough, the area was empty, and I wandered round disconsolately until I found a man behind a desk labelled 'Baggage Handling'.

I explained the nature of my problem, and gave him my baggage tags.

'Hold on for a few minutes, sir, and I'll see what I can find out.'

He disappeared for forty-five minutes, during which I never took my eyes off the luggage belt, just in case.

And then there he was, striding into the area carrying a suitcase. Mine!

I could have kissed it, and him.

'You'll never believe where we found it!' he said.

'Where?'

'On the runway! The baggage handlers must have taken it out, seen the fragile labels and put it aside, and then forgotten about it!'

'The runway? You mean, the real runway?'

'Yup!'

'Where a plane could have run them over?'

'I'm sure it wouldn't have come to that ...' he said, that little bit tentatively.

'PLANE CRASH CAUSED BY LONDON BOOKSELLER!'

I clutched my case firmly as I exited, and found my sister pacing about anxiously in the waiting area.

'What took you so long?' she asked.

Three days later, I upgraded my Virgin Atlantic ticket to London to Upper Class – we dealers for Texas travel well – in order to take my two carry-on bags, into which the books were now divided, on to the plane. We arrived safely at Heathrow in the morning, and I went straight to my office with my treasures.

The next months were, well, interesting. It's not all that easy to sell so many copies of *Ulysses*, having nine made them look that little bit common. These are rare books, are they? I took them to book fairs, and offered three of them (one of each issue, with a fetching colour picture) in my Catalogue 19. Within six months, though, they had sold: one private collector bought a copy of all three issues, while the others were purchased by a mix of private and trade buyers. Even at 20 per cent, I did very well out of it and Tom Staley was delighted.

I began planning another trip to Austin, because, from the onset, I'd had not two, but three reasons for proposing my, not exactly modest, but reasonable charge for selling the books. Yes, (1) it was fairer at that level; and yes, (2) I wanted Staley to be extra happy to see me next time; but also, (3) surely the de-acquisitioning of the Joyce items presaged a fuller, more extensive and more profitable clear out of Texas duplicates coming my way?

I spent a great deal of time scrutinising their online catalogue, and discovered a wide range of treasures: duplicates, and sometimes multiple copies, of many of the most expensive rare books of the nineteenth and twentieth centuries: more Joyce, a lot of TS Eliot and TE Lawrence, Darwin, Dickens, Dylan Thomas, the list went on and on. I wasn't going to get as rich as that viper Feldman, but prospects looked good.

Before my next visit to Texas, though, Tom arrived in London, on one of his many trips to see friends, examine archives, and bask in the English literary scene that he so enjoyed. We made an appointment for lunch, and he came round to my office/shop in Pied Bull Yard in Bloomsbury. He'd often visited, and he almost never looked at the books. Occasionally, I would pull something off the shelf, but he'd seen better and more interesting copies at home. And, as he was happy to admit, he wasn't all that interested in acquiring books; he read them avidly, and wrote a good few, but as Director of the HRC he was fixated on archives, letters and manuscripts.

Over lunch I brought up the question of whether we might do more business on the Texas duplicates, and I showed him my list of books that, surely, he could do without. He looked it over with a smile, but scant interest.

'That's all over now,' he said.

'No more de-accessioning?'

He nodded, yes. No more.

'What happened?'

'Well, when my staff heard about the *Ulysses* sales ...'– I'd rather suspected he'd done that more or less on his own – '... a number of them objected.' He gave a wry grimace.

'Why was that?'

'Oh, various reasons. Some of them objected in principle. Some because it wasn't a sufficiently transparent sale. Others because they believed that our duplicates should be offered to other Universities in Texas, because we're a state institution ...'

I was disappointed but not entirely surprised to hear this. We ate our lunch in amiable accord, finished the bottle of wine, and ordered dessert. His colleagues were probably right, and Tom said he had acceded gracefully, having little choice.

The general question thus remains: what should libraries do with their valuable duplicates? And so far as I can see, the answer is: keep them, it's easier that way. Though Tom was in a unique situation (there's no library in the world so over-stocked with multiple copies of rare books) it made some sense – but perhaps not enough – to monetise them. But it was clearly not worth the bother, and in libraries as in all forms of business, you have to pick your fights.

In the ensuing years I've never bought a library duplicate again. I don't mind. Like Dr Staley, my interest has increasingly been on archives, and there are no duplications there, and much more in the way of stimulation, as readers of this book will understand.

8

Who Gives a Damn about *Beedle the Bard*?

A unique copy of JK Rowling's The Tales of Beedle the Bard
will go on sale at Sotheby's auction house in London on 13
December 2007. The volume of previously untold handwritten
stories is expected to fetch up to £40,000 in a charity auction.
The *Guardian*, 11 November 2007

Next to us in the queue, a well brought-up and dressed-up
Islington boy, of just the right reading age, peered up at me
without a glimmer of condescension, as I put on my witch's
hat, and tried to fit the string under my beard.

'It looks a bit wonky,' he said, screwing up his eyes and
standing on tiptoes. 'It's tilted a bit to the left.'

I refrained from saying that everyone in Islington is tilted
to the left, though he was sufficiently precocious to have
understood.

I went on to one knee. 'Could you fix it?'

He took the commission seriously, moved the hat an inch
one way, stepped back and closed an eye to focus, adjusted and
readjusted it. Next to us, his mother and my daughter Anna

(age 29) offered advice and feedback. In hardly any time they were agreed that I looked spiffing, and was now entitled to partake of the sweeties that were being offered by the young lady from Waterstones on Islington Green.

It was 11.38 on a balmy Friday evening (20 June 2003), well past the bedtimes of the excited but well-behaved children in the queue, many of whom had dressed up as wizards, and were juddering in anticipation, as if awaiting the train arriving at Platform 9¾. It was the night of the gimmicky but rather agreeable midnight release of *Harry Potter and the Order of the Phoenix*, the fifth novel in the *Harry Potter* series. Waterstones' staff made sure that all the kids and their parents were equipped for the long wait. The young woman who arrived to give us our treats had a good look at me, then peered at Anna and her husband Steve, and behind them to locate their child. No such was apparent: for these purposes they were their own child. I was, too, if that makes any sense.

'Just the three of us, I'm afraid,' I said, yearning for my sweets, fighting off the desire to tip my witch's cap deferentially, and then finding it in need of readjusting. A wicker basket of multi-coloured jelly frogs and snakes was soon offered, and we studied it with care. My hat-fitter peered into the basket like a chess player over a board, till he had to be goaded by his mother. It was hard! Frog or snake? Which colour? He picked up an orange and a yellow frog, looked at them indecisively, and put the yellow one back. I took a yellow, and Anna and Steve both chose green. Once I was confident my little chum was happy with his choice, I popped mine in my mouth, remembering to suck rather than chew. I lose a lot of fillings to gummy sweets. When Anna was little we used to have contests to see who could suck a sweet, a dried apricot or a pickle, for the longest time without chewing and swallowing. She always won. She immediately challenged me to a gummy frog contest, and won that, too, as soon as mine was soft enough for safe biting.

At exactly midnight, as if by a magic spell, the doors of the shop sprang open and we piled in, to be met by a huge pile of books stacked in the front. We bought two. Anna was at that time, to my astonishment, chagrin, and (sort of) pride, a reporter for the *News of the World*, and had been tasked to review the new *Harry Potter* overnight so they could scoop the other papers – the first ever literary scoop of that godawful rag. Her diary caught something of the spirit of the night:

> *It was a lively atmosphere, with children and adults alike, speculating on who was going to be killed off and eating jelly frogs and snakes. At 12.45am, we had our copies and I head back to the office. Putting my feet up on the newsdesk, I started the book. At 7.00am I had finished it and written my review. When I left the office, I was so tired my head was spinning.*

Though the paper came out the next morning, by the time Anna filed it was too late, and when the next Sunday came round, all the other papers had already reviewed it. More droop than scoop.

I was then only halfway through the novel, and quite enjoying it in my leisurely fashion. I admired the *Harry Potters*, when I wasn't annoyed by their cutesified weirdness. As a child I favoured neither dungeons nor dragons, and hate magic realism as an adult. I prefer things as they are, and I feel

more secure when they stay that way. Unforeseen transforma-
tions, flitting from one mode of being to another, make me
irritable and anxious.

The *Harry Potters* were uneven in quality, viewed either
internally or on a book-by-book basis, but when they were
good they were terrific fun. The third in the series, *Harry
Potter and the Prisoner of Azkaban*, which introduces the terrifying figures of the Dementors, who suck your soul out, is
starkly terrifying, and if not of the quality of *Huckleberry Finn,
Alice in Wonderland*, or *His Dark Materials*, I find it equally
memorable. In spite of my academic background, my imagi-
nation and intellectual life are not entirely constructed on
categories of high and low, better or worse, serious or frivo-
lous, literary or popular. The key quality for entry into my
internal pantheon is adhesiveness. Some things stick, others
slide away.

If the children of the world adored Harry Potter, that was
a confirmation that he was worth taking seriously. He stuck.
But serious literary people, as they are called, frequently
demurred. In a scathing, forensic piece in the *New York Times*,
AS Byatt remarked that 'Ms Rowling's world has no place for
the numinous. It is written for people whose imaginative lives
are confined to TV cartoons ...' There's some truth in this,
but it didn't bother me for a moment. I love TV cartoons, one
of my abiding role models is Bugs Bunny, and if 'TV cartoons'
is meant to be disparaging, I wonder what Byatt makes of *The
Simpsons*, much the best thing written for telly in the last
twenty years. Rowling's admirers, of course, fought back,
accusing an envious Byatt of dumping a 'goblet of bile' on
Harry and his author. I rather agreed.

When the series ended with *The Deathly Hallows* in 2007, I, like millions of other readers, felt cast adrift. The final book masterfully knitted together and resolved multiple narratives, and was so satisfying that our disappointment multiplied. What could Rowling possibly do, not merely to extend, but to build upon the stories and audience that she had created? The answer lay in a small section of the final volume, which introduces a character called Beedle the Bard, who seemed no great shakes at the time he entered the fictional world, but who was to come into his own the very next year.

In the last will and testament of Albus Dumbledore, the late Headmaster of Hogwarts (I still can't believe she killed him!), a shabby leather volume entitled *The Tales of Beedle the Bard* was left to Hermione Granger. It was of great antiquity, in a binding 'stained and peeling in places', with the title on its cover, written in embossed runic symbols. It consisted of five short stories, none of which were printed in the text of *The Deathly Hallows*.

As we have learnt since she first appeared on the scene, if there is any rule that governs JK Rowling's writerly life it is 'keep going'. *Harry Potter and the Deathly Hallows* was published on 21 July 2007. *The Tales of Beedle the Bard* was published the next year. Yet *Beedle* entered the world not as a book but as a manuscript. Seven handwritten and illustrated manuscripts to be precise, one of which was offered for auction at Sotheby's, London, on 13 December 2007, as lot number 311A in their winter sale of books and manuscripts. The auctioneers issued an illustrated catalogue for this single item, which they estimated might fetch £30,000–£50,000. Since Rowling had no intention, at this point, of publishing the book, the buyer would be one of only seven people in the world with access to it. Or, I suppose, seven people and all the children of their acquaintance.

Rowling explained the genesis of the manuscript:

The idea came really because I wanted to thank six key people who have been very closely connected to the Harry Potter series, and these were people for whom a piece of jewellery wasn't going to cut it. So I had the idea of writing them a book, a handwritten and illustrated book, just for these six people. And well, if I'm doing six, I really have to do seven, and the seventh book will be for this cause, which is so close to my heart.

Copy Number 7, the 'Moonstone Edition', of 157 pages, went to auction on behalf of Rowling's Lumos Foundation, a charity supporting the care of children in orphanages. (Moonstones, Rowling noted, were representative of 'mothers, lovers and the power of dreams'.) Sotheby's had offered their services and facilities free of charge – the first time this had happened with a lot in a 'normal' sale rather than a stand-alone charity event – and put on a pre-sale reception distinctly swanky even by their standards. The occasion was worth its weight in publicity gold, the room filled with TV cameras, paparazzi, and news reporters. Oh, and us in the audience, virtually none of whom had any interest in bidding on the item, or the means to pay for it if we had.

At the party on the night preceding the sale, Belinda and I were each given a copy of the attractively produced blue-covered catalogue, and I soon queued to have ours signed by Rowling for my children. In her haste and my confusion, I'd handed her the books upside-down, which is how her signature thus appeared.

'Oooh lovely!' I said. 'Is this your magic signature, with a special significance?'

'Nope,' she said, and smiled. 'Sorry!' and carried on signing.

'It is now!' I said, as I tucked my treasures in my jacket pocket.

I soon gave the special copies with the magical (extra valuable!) upside-down signature to the kids, who were mildly diverted by them. Being the world's most peripatetic person, my wildlife photographer son Bertie lost his, indeed he has no memory of it; Anna, on the other hand, who is bookish and relatively stationary, can find hers in a second, and was astonished to hear it is now worth £1,000. I haven't told Bertie.

But if Rowling could add extra value merely with a wonky signature, how much – we were all speculating – might something as, well, bulky and gaudy and eye-catching, as the Beedle manuscript be worth?

'The problem,' I explained confidently to an audience of three as we drank our champagne at the reception, 'is that no one knows how much the damn thing is worth. No Rowling manuscript material has yet come on the market, neither genuine working material, nor things like this *Beedle*, which is basically just a made-up gewgaw.'

I later learnt that a Rowling item of a similar sort, a 31-page manuscript with illustrations entitled *Hogwarts School of Witchcraft and Wizardry*, a handmade 'miniature book' of 2.4 x 1.6 inches, had sold for £10,000 at charity auction in 2004.

The sale never entered *Book Auction Records*, but Sotheby's clearly knew about it, hence their modest pre-sale estimate.

'So,' said one of my audience, 'let's have a guess at what it will fetch!'

'A hundred to one-fifty,' I said confidently. 'What do you think?'

One of our group was Dotti Irvine, Head of Colman Getty, who do the PR for many major events, like the Booker Prize.

'A million pounds!' said Dotti.

The second guesser was Belinda.

'Eight hundred thousand,' she said.

Amateurs!

'There's no *Harry Potter* collector who'd pay anything like that,' I scoffed.

'I know,' said Dotti. 'We'll just have to see.'

The next day, people began to take their seats, the auctioneer glided on to the rostrum, and a variety of swish Sotheby's representatives manned a bank of telephones, ready for calls from absent bidders. I looked round the room, but Rowling, who had been busily signing copies of the book the night before, was nowhere to be seen. I asked a friend of mine from Sotheby's where she'd gone.

'Home,' he said, 'she was worried that it might not fetch within the estimate, and fail to sell,' he said, 'so she's following the sale from Edinburgh.' This didn't make any sense, of course. It was certainly going to sell. Even I would have paid £40,000 for it. But had she stayed, all eyes would have been on her, which would've been horrid.

The bidding on Lot 311A began at £30,000. Feeling safe from any possibility of purchase, I put my hand up, just to be on telly, but there were lots of other hands up for the same reason. The auctioneer moved smoothly up to a bid of £240,000, with several buyers interested, and there was a distinct pause. I looked round the room for Dotti, so I could give her my piercing 'I told you so' look. By the time I located the back of her head, the bidding had resumed, alternating now between someone on the phone and a man in a suit standing nonchalantly at the back of the room. Sotheby's were later to reveal that there had been six active bidders, though they didn't reveal at what level they were bidding. Perhaps I was one of them.

You measure the progress of an item at auction by following the rise of the increments between bids. Up to £100,000 we were proceeding in increments of £10,000. Soon this leapt to £20,000 as the relentless bidders carried on and on. Soon the increments were £50,000. Then £100,000. The crowd had gasped and gossiped at first, but had now grown silent.

'One million, six hundred thousand pounds ...

'One million, seven hundred thousand pounds ...

'One million, eight hundred thousand pounds ...

'One million, nine hundred thousand pounds ...'

There was a distinct change of atmosphere in the room, which seemed all of a sudden to have less air in it. Were we going to reach two million pounds? And then there was a pause.

'One million nine-fifty!' came the next bid, perhaps an indication of a final attempt. The auctioneer accepted the bid, and looked about the room, as if searching for a third party who might have been lying in wait. He didn't look my way.

'I'm selling now,' he said, raising his gavel in the air, 'last chance, any advance on one million, nine hundred and fifty thousand pounds?'

'Bang' went the gavel.'Whoosh' went the air from hundreds of lungs. And a round of applause began, and escalated, and carried on. I was moved, in spite of myself – I loathe applause at auctions when a rich person buys something for a ton of money – but after all this was for charity, and all of us had a sense of having participated in something both memorable and worthy.

And what a price! At the pertaining exchange rate, it came to almost $4 million. It was not only the most expensive children's item ever sold, but also the most expensive modern literary manuscript. Twice the price of Kafka's *The Trial*! It needed some explanation, I felt, above and beyond the unhelpful shrug: charity auction!

Still slightly shocked, but glowing, Rowling was being interviewed in Edinburgh by a cluster of journalists, and said the obvious things:'I am stunned and ecstatic. This will mean so much to children in desperate need of help. It means Christmas has come early for me.'

It had for Sotheby's, too. The auction and its aftermath became news round the world. In their press release, Philip Errington, Deputy Director of the Books and Manuscripts department said:'Sotheby's has been thrilled to work with JK Rowling and The Children's Voice in selling this wonderful manuscript. This is one of the most exciting pieces of children's literature to have passed through Sotheby's. We have to reach back eighty years to find a comparison when we sold the manuscript of *Alice's Adventures in Wonderland* on behalf of the original Alice.'

Belinda and I soon made our way out into Bond Street, and started the walk north to our flat in Marylebone, discussing the sale. She didn't rub it in that she'd been a hell of a lot closer to the price than I was.

'Well,' I said, a trifle defensively. 'It was a charity auction, prices can be off the charts, we still don't really know what it's worth ...'

She looked at me quizzically. That had been her point all along.

'... so we won't be able to make that judgement until we know what just happened, and why. Perhaps we never will. But until you interrogate the data, you don't know how to learn from it ...'

The bare outlines of the story soon emerged. The book had been purchased by the St James's art dealers Hazlitt, Gooden and Fox (whose representative had been in the sale-room) on behalf of Amazon. Fair enough. If Jeff Bezos wanted the book, he could buy it with his small change, and had presumably instructed his agent simply to purchase it, without setting a limit. Why he wanted it was unstated. Perhaps one of his children was a Harry fanatic?

Bezos, at this point, wasn't giving anything away, and issued an anodyne press release:

> *Even before establishing her charity, JK Rowling had done the world a rare and immeasurably valuable service — enlarging forever our concept of the way books can touch people — and in particular children — in modern times.*

According to the Reuters report the day after the sale, Amazon.com had already 'posted several pictures of the book – which it handles with white gloves – and posted a review of one tale called 'The Wizard and the Hopping Pot' on their website, noting that 'the company plans to post reviews of all five tales'. Soon enough, the manuscript was reported to be on display in a vitrine in the entrance to the Amazon offices, with two armed guards beside it, prior to its travels to promote its proud, and canny, new owners.

The inexorable Amazon machine was so quickly into action that it was retrospectively obvious that Mr Bezos intended to acquire Mr Beedle whatever the price, promising 'a permanent link would direct interested parties to http://www.amazon.com/beedlebard'. (Try following it now: permanently gone!) The site soon posted several high-quality pictures and a video, with someone reading the note from JK Rowling that was printed inside the cover. Amazon.com editors were immediately taking questions about the tales on the site's discussion boards. Making a virtue of necessity, Amazon announced that they would respect copyright: 'It won't be publishing the book unless JK Rowling decides to do so, but it will be taking the book on tour to schools and libraries so children can see it themselves.' There were rumours at the time that Amazon had offered a chance for selected readers to actually spend time with the manuscript, and apparently there was a public reading of it. Neither, it was claimed, involved an infringement of copyright.

This being the Internet, there were grouchy voices as well. A site called Vulture.com posted a complaint from an aggrieved Rowling enthusiast, who felt disenfranchised by all these fancy goings-on: 'But if she really wanted to create a charitable windfall, she should have sold *Beedle the Bard* in stores . . . And we maintain that it's a poor thank-you to your fans to write a book and then refuse to let anyone read it, other than the glove-wearing employees of the rich corporation who outbid everyone else.' The Internet was soon chock-a-block with similarly disgruntled *Harry* aficionados, bemoaning the fact that a millionaire could afford to read *Beedle*, but that normal folk were excluded.

The details have never emerged. Rowling relented. A few months later the trade edition of *The Tales of Beedle the Bard* was in the bookshops, but not, significantly, available through Amazon. There was some gossip, probably reliable but difficult to substantiate, that Rowling and Mr Bezos were involved in litigation, as she argued that Amazon must desist in its (mis) use of her text, and he argued back at great length and cost. Whatever the result, it was so hemmed in by confidentiality agreements that virtually nothing was revealed, even on the Internet. My friends at Sotheby's said they knew nothing about it.

Only Sotheby's knew who the under-bidder was, and he presumably had a 'buy' commission as well, until he chickened out. Or perhaps he had a limit of two million. Rumours suggested that the under-bidder was representing 'someone from the Middle East', who apparently had a daughter who was mad on Harry. I hope the representative didn't get in trouble when he decided to stop bidding: *I didn't send you to not buy the damn book!* Might it have been for MBS? Voldemort himself!

After such a remarkable experience in the book/manuscript marketplace, I found myself asking: What is to be learnt at the feet of this *Beedle*? It was a remarkable price. Was it worth it? Is that, therefore, its value? The answer is of course both yes and no. On the night, that's what it fetched. On some future night would it fetch as much? Almost certainly not.

The story helps to explain why I, after some thirty years as a dealer in rare books, more or less gave it up. Manuscripts are more fun, riskier, harder to market and to get right. There's something a trifle stolid about books, even the best and rarest of them: value-wise you know where you are. How much is a first folio of Shakespeare worth? Find out how much the previous few sold for, compare them on grounds of condition, and you will more or less be able to say how much the next one might fetch.

In my preferred new world of manuscripts and archives, though, the process of comparison and prognostication is by no means so straightforward. At the simplest level there are single letters and individual manuscripts. How much is a good DH Lawrence letter worth? Or a manuscript of a Dylan Thomas poem? You can look that up, and work it out, and get not a single figure but a range of values. (Lawrence: £300–£3,000, depending on content and recipient; Dylan: £500–£5,000, depending on which poem, and whether it is a working or a fair copy.) So far, so easy.

But we're still a long way from our pesky *Beedle*, sitting like a gilded millionaire at the top of this manuscript mountain. It was a ludicrous price. On the night it was worth it, because it happened: it was transactionally driven. Willing seller, willing buyer, justified price. But what factors contributed to its elephantiasis? There were a few: Rowling-mania considered generally, Sotheby's capacity to generate interest in an unknown and never to be published item, the fact that it was an auction on behalf of deprived children ... no, nope, not enough. What made for the galactic price were those most welcome of all figures in an auction house: a rabidly determined buyer and an (almost) equally determined under-bidder. We had one of each, and thus the figures: £2 million, $4 million.

The obvious question? What would one of the six other manuscript copies of *Beedle* fetch if it came up at auction? If the 2007 *Beedle* price has to be described as uniquely trans-actional, how much would a later copy be worth? Admittedly, a second copy would be offered after publication of the book, whereas at the first time of offering it was claimed that a book was not going to be published. But any of the further six *Beedle*s still in private hands would benefit from the earlier price, if one came up for sale. What would the next one fetch?

The answer was bound to come, sooner or later, as the gravitational pull of that remarkable 2007 auction kicked in, and pound signs flashed in front of the eyes of the six lucky owners (who had never been named, though one could certainly guess the majority). And, sure enough, in 2016 one of them came forward.

This copy was inscribed to Barry Cunningham, who was the publisher (at Bloomsbury) who bought *Harry Potter and the Philosopher's Stone*. The inscription reads: 'To Barry, the man who thought an overlong novel about a boy wizard in glasses might just sell ... THANK YOU!' Cunningham loved the book from the start, but was severely realistic about its chances of success. Bloomsbury only published 500 copies of the first edition (most of which went to libraries), and over a modest celebratory lunch, Cunningham warned Rowling that 'she would never make any money from her book'.

His manuscript copy was also bound in leather, but this time the gems were rhodochrosite, 'traditionally associated with love, balance, and joy in daily life'. Sotheby's now knew more or less what they were dealing with, and had a shrewd idea of how the market might respond. The book had been published years before, which would have a major effect on the value of yet another manuscript. Their pre-sale estimate for the sale was £300,000–£500,000. Pretty much spot on: it sold for £368,750.

I wonder if Mr Cunningham was pleased or disappointed? And how much will the next copy – for there will surely be one – fetch at auction? But I've had enough of this dratted Beedle: frankly, my dear, I don't give a damn.

9

The Protocols of the Elders of Zionism

Two original drafts of the Balfour Declaration, part of the highly important Zionist Archive of Leon Simon, which also includes a signed letter from Chaim Weizmann asking his colleagues to review the draft, and further documents concerning the formulation of the Balfour Declaration, and of the British Mandate in Palestine.
Manchester, London, Palestine: 1917–1922, 1937–1944.

Estimate: *$500,000–$800,000.*

Provenance: *Sir Leon and Lady Ellen Simon — Purchased from the estate of Miss Aviva Simon (daughter of the above).*

Provenance? Ha! They were mine. Or half of them were. Or perhaps 20 per cent . . . or 45 per cent. It depended on whom you asked, and how, and (particularly) when.

★

143

'House clearance'. There's something ineffably melancholy about the very term. Someone has died, their house must be sold, but first it needs to be emptied. Various relatives and friends enter, walk about mournfully, snuffle discreetly, think the requisite deep thoughts, then choose a few photographs and letters, try on an occasional piece of jewellery, consider the furniture, pluck a few pictures from the walls and books from the shelves. Consider the carpets, and reject most. Are there any lamps or fixtures worth taking?

Surely, surely, there's something ... there might be something ... What is it? ... Where is it? You read about it, see it on telly, hear breathless gasps: someone has found something! Something that they didn't even know was of value, and it's worth a *lot* of money. It might be an unprepossessing Chinese pot, a begrimed painting by an Old Master, a gaudy egg – that old thing? We had it on a kitchen shelf! ... such treasures pop up occasionally in people's lives.

Except mine. And yours. Looking at the ever popular, fantasy-feeding and enhancing *Antiques Roadshow*, you'd swear that, surely, there must be something at Aunt Jenny's (she had such good taste!) ... One really must go round for a little ... peep ... before the old girl pops it, and the house clearance people cart the goodies off to Sotheby's.

I am a relatively high-end bookseller; my shelves rarely display more than a few hundred books. As far as I'm concerned, 'inventory' is merely another term for the books you can't sell. I chose this area of the market both because I am attracted to unique, and uniquely valuable books, but also because I am luxuriously indolent, and want to have fun. Real booksellers, proper ones with shops and rooms full of shelved books, are used to schlepping their inventory from place to place, filling multiple cartons and occasional vans full of stock, emptying them, and starting again. Hard work.

Consequently I am rarely asked to clear the books from someone's deceased relative's house. But of course it happens. If the previous owner was a sufficiently ambitious acquirer of books, or was merely in the right places at the right times, then I will go and have a look. Over the last forty years I've done so with the books previously owned by many writers, academics and luminaries, and the ensuing conversation is always the same.

'Well,' I will say to the seller, 'I'm afraid these are not all for me. But I have pulled out a few books that I can give you more for than if I took the entire lot.'

'Why is that?'

'Because the cost and effort of taking them all is not worth it to me. But I can put you in touch with dealers who will give you a fair price for the rest, though be warned that second-hand books are of little value ...'

'So why would they take them?'

'They put them in shops and on the Internet, which is a huge effort, but over the years they presumably make a profit, or they wouldn't keep doing it.'

In no time at all I have bought my small handful of books, recommended a couple of reliable booksellers with big muscles and bigger vans, and gone on my way.

On 25 March 2003, Aviva Simon died in London. Her house in 154 Hanover Road, NW10 was overflowing with books, documents, and associated material, much of which was formerly owned by her late father, the distinguished Zionist

Leon (later Sir Leon) Simon. Once the family had cleared whatever possessions they wished to keep, there was the overwhelming problem of the many thousands of books and papers. Sotheby's and Christie's were called in, but neither was excited by the material, for reasons which will become clear.

It was a large Edwardian house in Willesden, stuffed with the residue of the life's work of several distinguished members of the family. A house clearance man had come to assess the situation, was horrified, and never seen again. Subsequently, the executor of the estate called a North London Hassidic book dealer, who dealt with his partner under the name ML Books, inquiring if they might like to buy the material. In December and January 2003–04, the firm visited the house and began the massive undertaking, because the owners insisted that, aside from a case containing family photographs which had been set aside, 'taking everything is part of the deal'. A lorry load was taken away. It snowed overnight and eventually a second lorry was loaded. The dealers paid £3,000 for the lot, and on 28 January received a handwritten receipt on a scrap of paper indicating a sale of books and miscellaneous material, signed by the appointed representative of the estate.

Even by the trying standards of house clearances, this was a nightmare. Poor Mr Landau, of ML books, was later to recall that, after the labour of packing and transporting the cartons, 'We unpacked everything after hours and hours of work, took it back to our office which was packed to the ceiling with all this stuff. We still had to go back for more ...'

To dispose of very large quantities of material, you need to divide it into categories: first, the things you want to keep for inventory, then you break up the unwanted stuff into further sections, and find bookselling colleagues to buy the various bits. The London Judaica dealer Jonathan Fishburn was thus enlisted to buy the Zionist pamphlets, on the condition he help clear all of the 'non-Jewish' books, which he passed on to yet another trade colleague. A few months later, after having purchased and dispersed a very great number of books, Jonathan suggested that it was essential that the buyers obtain a formal and more specific receipt for the clearance, written on letter-headed paper, properly dated and signed by the executor, not by his representative. On 27 July they received the following, signed by David Landman:

> *This is to confirm that a quantity of books, pamphlets, letters and ephemeral material (mostly Judaica and Zionist history) at one time the property of Sir Leon and of Dr AJV Underwood was purchased by ML Books of 52A Windus Road, 5–6 Star Mews, London N16 6UP, from David Landman, executor of the estate of the late Aviva Nesta Simon of 154 Hanover Street, London NW10.*

This was more precise and more formal than the previous scrappy receipt.

The major outstanding problem for ML Books was now the disposal of dozens of red box files containing miscellaneous papers and letters, formerly the property of Leon Simon. They did not specialise in such material, and soon sold it to Harold 'Shlomo' Breuer, a New York Judaica dealer, who also had premises in London.

He is the hero of this story. On first examination of the contents of the box files, it was clear to him that most of the material was unsaleable, but more importantly that the most historically interesting and valuable items were variously located, some in one box, others in others. The reason that Christie's and Sotheby's experts had originally declined what was later called the 'Balfour archive' was that there was no such thing. It required the assiduous, percipient research of Shlomo Breuer not to locate the Balfour archive, but to create it.

After weeks of toil, he put together the 600-odd pages of material that centred round Simon's involvement with the Balfour Declaration. He offered this for sale to two leading American Judaica dealers, both of whom turned it down. It was only at this point that he asked Jonathan Fishburn, who'd been so active in helping ML Books to sell off so much lesser material, if he might be interested.

At this early stage in his bookselling career Jonathan's taste – he saw immediately that the newly curated papers were of great historical interest – rather exceeded his means, so he rang me to see if I might be interested in buying them with him. Though the newly created file was stuffed with papers various and interesting, he understood that only one page of them was crucial, and that was Simon's working notes on the formulation of the declaration, which were sent for approval by Lord Balfour, the Foreign Secretary.

Would I like to see it? Of course! Not that I knew much about it. My academic and bookselling background is literary. When I think of 1917, I think of the books that were published that year: *Prufrock*, *To the Lighthouse*, *The Wild Swans at Coole*, *Look! We Have Come Through!*, *The Shadow Line* ... If you dragged me outside this comfort zone, I could probably place the Russian revolution in the same year, and I suppose the historical proclamation under discussion.

The Balfour Declaration? My mind went, if not blank, certainly cloudy. A few facts floated to the surface. Palestine? Mmmm; foundation document for the State of Israel? Hmmmm. But as to its contents, or the inwardness of its drafting and effect, nothing at all. Before going off to see the papers, I did enough googling to fill in a few mmmms and hmmms, and had for a brief moment a rough idea of what the Balfour Declaration was, and why unknown early iterations of it might be of immense historical interest.

Born the son of a Manchester Rabbi in 1881, Leon Simon attended Balliol College, Oxford, and became a Hebraist, scholar, and ardent Zionist, and an influential member of the Manchester circle that included the charismatic Chaim Weizmann, later to become the first President of Israel. The papers that Shlomo Breuer had painstakingly assembled give a complete view of Simon's role, not merely in drafting the penultimate version of the Declaration, but detailing the story through the next five years, with documentation of the many arguments both for and against the annexation of Palestine.

Historically valuable, to be sure. And certainly valuable in the marketplace. But how valuable?

When I arrived at Shlomo's house, I was greeted warmly, and introduced to his rather shy wife and lovely children, who soon left us to it. I was offered and gratefully drank a glass of water. He had put the folder on the table, and I sat down to go through it. Which I didn't. I am, I suppose, the opposite of Shlomo Breuer, who has a great eye for detail, and the patience to sift through material diligently. I want to see the best things, and I prefer to see them now. After I'd leafed through some modestly interesting material, I came upon the pages that made the deal compelling.

The first, a working draft towards a Declaration, was written by Harry Sacher, of the Manchester *Guardian*, and presented to the 17 July 1917 London meeting where eight members of the Zionist Political Committee met. In this version he had suggested a 'National Home' rather than a 'Jewish State', including the concept of a 'chartered company' that would empower the Zionists to purchase land and initiate development projects.

What finally emerged was far more radical. The second and most interesting item was written by Leon Simon on the letter-headed stationery of the Imperial Hotel on Russell Square in London. It contained only two sentences:

H[is] M[ajesty's] G[overnment] accepts the principle that Palestine should be reconstituted as the Nat[ional] Home of the J[ewish] P[eople]. HMG will use its best efforts to secure the achievement of this object, and will discuss the necessary methods and means with the Z[ionist] O[rganization].

This was regarded as something of a bombshell even at the time, and bombs of a power unimaginable in 1917 are still dropping today. If Palestine was the aspirational homeland of the Jews, it was the actual homeland of the soon-to-be-displaced population of millions.

Concern about such repercussions informs the final text of Balfour's proclamation, which read:

His Majesty's Government view with favour the establishment of a national home for the Jewish people, and will use their best endeavours to facilitate the achievement of this object, it being clearly understood that nothing shall be done which may prejudice the civil and religious rights of existing non-Jewish communities in Palestine, or the rights and political status enjoyed by Jews in any other country.

After reading Simon's draft and reflecting upon its monumental consequences – it would be naïve to call them unforeseen – I was pleased to write a cheque for £22,000 to buy the material. Shlomo gave me a signed receipt dated 17 June 2004.

How did I know that the papers were buyable at this price? I didn't, not quite. But in situations where I'm having a bit of a punt, I ask myself two questions: will I lose money by paying the asking price? And at what higher price would I walk away? I thought it inconceivable that I could lose money by paying £22,000; I would not have written a cheque for £50,000, but asked for a few days to consider, and to consult further reference works, auction records, and colleagues more knowledgeable than I (it would have been difficult to find any less knowledgeable). At £100,000 I would have shrugged my shoulders and departed.

Knowing all too little about the market for such weighty historical documents, Jonathan and I soon took the papers for appraisal at Sotheby's in London. Their experts were immediately engaged and excited, suggested that the sale take place in New York (more wealthy Jews?), and provided a provisional estimate of £150,000, a nice confirmation of Jonathan's acuity. We soon showed Sotheby's lawyers the documentation for the original sale. Was the provenance adequate? Absolutely. Was it perfectly clear that title (that is, ownership) had passed? Certainly. In the ensuing months an export licence was applied for and granted, and the material was catalogued and offered as Lot 217 for the forthcoming Fine Books and Manuscripts sale at Sotheby's, New York, on 16 June 2005. Their description of the papers included the following pitch:

> *If the Declaration of Independence can be viewed as the first formal political step in the foundation of the United States, then the Balfour Declaration can be so viewed in the history of Israel, and the present memorandum is the equivalent of an autograph draft of the text by Thomas Jefferson.*

Hyperbole is an auctioneer's version of understatement. This description beggars belief, or even credulity. The equivalent of a handwritten draft, by Thomas Jefferson, of the Declaration of Independence! That would be worth $10 million, and rising ... But these drafts of the Balfour Declaration are not in the hand even of Chaim Weizmann, who was sent the draft for comment, but were written by the relatively obscure Leon Simon, newly crowned as the Thomas Jefferson of Israel by the auctioneers.

Reading this exuberant catalogue entry, Jonathan and I were torn between conflicting sentiments, ranging from 'Oh my God, it's probably worth seven figures to the characteristically American dismissive formulation 'Go tell it to the Marines!' Yet, after all, it is for such over-reaching rhetorical chutzpah that one goes to Sotheby's in the first place.

A few days after the distribution of the catalogue, and an ensuing two-page spread about the sale in the *Independent*, lawyers for members of the Simon family contacted Sotheby's to deny that the catalogued material had been sold at all: the Hasidic dealers who did the house clearance had been instructed to take away only the books, not any documents. (The irony being that ML Books did not want the documents, which were stuffed in a closet in filthy old box files, but had been specifically instructed to take them away.) Sotheby's immediately backed down on their unambiguous assurances to Jonathan and myself, and said that unless we could sort this out with the Aviva Simon estate, the sale would be cancelled.

'Lawyers' – if there is a term that I find as unsettling as 'house clearance', that would be it. We needed one, and Jonathan had a quick solution in the person of one Henry Frydenson, whom he knew from his local *schul*, and who worked at the well-regarded London firm of Berwin Leyton Paisner. The latter of whom, Martin Paisner, was a sophisticated book collector, so I supposed that his colleague would know whom to consult if the intricacies of book dealing evaded him.

'You'll like him,' said Jonathan confidently. 'He's very bright. And very aggressive.'

That sounded just the ticket. Not only had we been abandoned by Sotheby's at the first whiff of trouble, we were being accused of dealing in material that had been wrongfully and perhaps wittingly removed from its premises. Perhaps by mistake, perhaps not.

Jonathan and I soon met Henry Frydenson, who was much as described, with a terrier-like appetite for opposition. We went through the details of the story, and showed him the documentation we had received.

'You've certainly got a strong case,' he said.

'I'll bet you say that to all the girls,' I replied, more concisely than is my wont, because when you're with an expensive lawyer time is money. When Henry opened our frequent further meetings by inquiring politely how I was, I'd say, 'Don't ask,' and moved to item 1 of our day's agenda.

The Simon family, too, had lawyered up, and soon presented the argument that the transaction had never included, or been intended to include, the documents at issue – the 'papers were not sold to Mr Weiser ... insofar as the papers were removed from the property, they were removed wrongfully'. Indeed, the lawyers continued, Mr Weiser has been 'warned off' removing the papers and documents 'on three separate occasions', which Mr Weiser strongly denied.

Well! There were a huge number of documents in the house, and it is unclear why the executors did not notice they were missing once the clearance had been completed, particularly as the dozens of box files were removed in the presence of the representative of the executor. Nor did they ever mention the documents until the catalogue was distributed by Sotheby's many months later. And of course there was the second receipt acknowledging the sale of documents, which had been signed and given to ML Books.

Henry Frydenson was scornful about this submission, responding to our antagonists that 'the version of facts set out in your letter is completely untenable', and demonstrating in detail why this was. It seemed ridiculous to me, but we would now have to sue the estate for title to the property. Henry soon instructed Emily Campbell as counsel, a distinctly crisp and highly intelligent young barrister, who after careful study and consideration, informed us that we had 'an extremely persuasive case'.

'How strong is it?' I asked.

'I would assess the chances of a judgment in our favour are 90 per cent. But – there's always a "but" in cases before the High Court – you never can tell what may happen on the day, or before which judge ...'

She paused for a moment, to get the next sentence right. 'On the one side you have a very distinguished Jewish family, and on the other ...' She didn't need to finish – two Jewish *dealers*. You get the wrong judge with the right stereotypes, and you're in trouble. The English suspicion of trade is deeply and widely held. Wordsworth put it succinctly in his general condemnation of commerce: 'Getting and spending, we lay waste our powers,' though how he obtained his pens and writing paper is thus uncertain.

The ensuing legal debates, involving acrimonious claims and counter-claims, and enough expenditure to buy an elephant and take it on holiday, eventually resulted in a meeting in Frydenson's office, in which the executors and some family from the Simon estate, together with their lawyers, were present. Before they were invited in from the waiting room, in which they'd been twiddling their thumbs, Henry turned to me, strictly. 'Not a word!' he admonished. 'Leave this entirely to me!'

As the Simon estate representatives trooped in silently and found places round the table, I studied their expressions carefully.

After all, these were in many ways my people, intellectual London Jews who had presumably led responsible and worthy lives. If they had made a mistake, it was not in selling the various documents so cheaply, but in failing adequately to research and to value them. They had tried, called in the major auction houses, and been told repeatedly that the material was of no significant value. They'd needed a Shlomo Breuer to find otherwise.

I should have been angry about the trouble and expense that their insubstantial claim, which even now I hesitate to call 'greedy', was causing myself and Jonathan, but my major feeling was that it was a sad occasion, and a cause of renewed grief and family recrimination. I felt sorry for them. I didn't say so. I didn't say anything.

Their lead lawyer began by suggesting a settlement.

'What do you propose?' asked Henry.

'I think that the sale should go ahead, and that we take 60 per cent, and your clients take 40 per cent ...'

Henry interrupted him. Taking the second and final sale receipt from the file in front of him, he passed it to the executor David Landman, who had signed it.

'Is this your signature?'

'Yes.' Landman had previously stated through his attorneys that he had no memory of having signed the letter, but the evidence was irrefutable, and he honoured it.

Henry reared up.

'You're wasting my time!' he said. 'Get out of my office!'

Our puzzled opponents looked at each other quizzically. Jonathan and I did, too, and cringed. Presumably this was some sort of legal slang, analogous to 'Get out of my face!'?

Their lawyer tried to intervene. 'We are here in good faith to negotiate a settlement,' he said, fully aware that Frydenson was indeed intent on showing them the door, 'and we will certainly listen sympathetically to any counter-suggestion. Perhaps a split of fifty-fifty?'

Henry rose to show them the door, pointed to it in case they didn't recognise one when they saw it, and opened it.

'Out!'

Within a few minutes they had all shuffled off, variously and rightly bemused, angry, and dumbfounded.

Noticing our chagrin, Henry said, 'It had to be done. Don't worry, it'll come out well in the end.' Jonathan had initially described Frydenson as 'very aggressive', which was turning out to be an understatement. He'd also labelled him 'very bright'. As we left the meeting, we wondered whether what we'd just witnessed was indeed bright. Or was it stupid?

Might they retaliate in kind, refuse further negotiations towards a settlement, and cause the cancellation of the auction until the High Court determined to whom the material belonged? That might have worked if they'd believed sufficiently in their own case. But they presumably were not in it to win the entire pot, which was unlikely, but to split it. The questions remained: how much would they take? How much were we prepared to give?

From our point of view, too, some minimal settlement might be necessary in order to ensure the auction went ahead. If we allowed the matter to drag on into the courts, and we (90 per cent likely) won, we might even have recovered our (burgeoning) legal costs. But that entailed the double risk of a (10 per cent likely) loss plus their costs, and the cancellation of the auction that would certainly have an adverse effect on the eventual value of the material. Potential buyers wouldn't know the details, but a cancelled sale frequently indicates problems with provenance or title.

Thus any future auction might carry question marks that would likely translate into a sale at a lower level. Once it became public that – a fact that Sotheby's felt unnecessary to mention – the 'archive' had actually been pieced together by Shlomo Breuer, it might have caused a degree of scepticism. Though, as any historian will testify, many archives and historical records are similarly knitted together from disparate sources. But there's something attractive about the notion that it was Leon Simon himself who had selected and preserved this record.

So it was in both parties' interest for the sale to proceed as scheduled, and to agree this before word got out – as it tends to do – and suspicion arose that there was something not strictly kosher about the title to the documents, and thus about the forthcoming sale. A week before it was due to take place, both parties agreed with Sotheby's that the auction of item 217 could go ahead, and the resulting proceeds be held in an escrow account until a settlement was reached, and the monies distributed.

Jonathan and I spent the ensuing weeks in (fruitless) speculation about how well the sale would do. Jonathan, who was unused to deals at this level, veered from pessimism (it won't even reach its reserve price!) to spurts of optimism prompted in part by an article in Jerusalem's *The Jewish Forward* noting that 'private collectors and institutions in Israel, Europe and America already have expressed interest'. (Surely the State of Israel has to buy it!)

Sotheby's kept bigging it up. The Head of their Books and Manuscripts department, David Redden, picked up the analogy with the Declaration of Independence, observing that the Balfour draft 'is almost like notes taken on the night of 3 July 1776', though he wisely omitted reference to Thomas Jefferson. The item soon figured in various dispatches from news agencies. Word had certainly got out.

Jonathan decided that he would get out, too, and scheduled a trip to New York to attend the sale. Mobile phones are not merely allowed but encouraged during the course of an auction, as bidders take instructions from their clients, so he could ring me a few minutes before Lot 217 came up, and I could listen as the bidding proceeded.

'OK,' he said from the saleroom, after we'd passed the time of day. 'We've just finished Lot 214, it will come up in a couple of minutes . . .'

'One question, Jonathan . . .'

'What's that?'

'How many people are on the phones?'

This was crucial. During an auction, members of Sotheby's staff sit to one side of the room in a bank of chairs behind a long table, phones to their ears talking with clients who may be bidding. With items of the highest value and the greatest interest, especially of international interest, the more people on the phone lines, the better an item might do. It is the only signifier of the likely depth of interest that a person in the auction room might observe.

'Four.'

'OK,' I said, 'let's hope for the best . . .'

It was a disappointing number – I've been to sales with fifteen people on the phones – but not a critical one.

The auctioneer soon announced, in a rasping voice: 'Lot 217. Two original drafts of the Balfour Declaration from the archive of Sir Leon Simon. There's a lot of interest in this. Who'll start me at five hundred thousand dollars?'

There was a pause as he looked round the room. It seemed to go on for ever.

This was the low estimate, and if there was interest, no one was yet showing their hand. This often happens. The reserve had been set, as is often the case, at 20 per cent below low estimate. So once a bid of $400,000 was in play, we had a certain sale.

'Four hundred thousand dollars then. Do I hear four hundred thousand dollars?'

He did.

Jonathan whispered, 'Thank God for that!'

The bids increased in increments of $20,000. Soon enough, $500,000 was reached, and the pace slowed somewhat.

'Any action on the phones?' I asked.

'Not yet …'

Phone bidders tend to wait until they sense the end is nigh, often operating under the misconception that if you come in on the bidding later you'll be likely to get a better price.

We'd reached $620,000 by now, and from what Jonathan could observe, there were only two active bidders. That's enough. An aggressive under-bidder can make all the difference. Did we have one?

The price inched up (when the increments are $20,000

those are valuable inches!), stalled for a bit, and then reached $775,000, as the auctioneer accepted a last bid at a smaller increment.

'I have seven hundred and seventy-five thousand dollars then. One more bid, sir? Any increase on seven hundred and seventy-five thousand dollars? Fair warning! I'm selling now at seven hundred and seventy-five thousand dollars ...'

Bang! The gavel went down. Jonathan breathed a long sigh of relief.

'That's OK then,' he said, 'near enough top estimate. What do you think?'

'I think you should go out for a drink and a good meal! I'm certainly going to. And enjoy the rest of your trip.'

But it was premature to celebrate. There was our High Court case still to be decided, in which the spoils might go one way, or the other, or both. As the trial date got closer, Frydenson wrote on our behalf to the defendants, suggesting a settlement. We took Emily Campbell's assessment of the risks as a working hypothesis: if we were 90 per cent likely to win, then that was more or less what we should claim. After some discussion, our antagonists accepted an offer of $100,000. Even after paying their lawyers, the rest was not a negligible sum (except compared to what Jonathan and I would get) and it was presumably not worth the considerable risk of a defeat, with costs, in the High Court.

When we deducted Sotheby's seller's commission, the agreed settlement to the Aviva Simon Estate, and Henry Frydenson's bill, Jonathan and I would each receive a very substantial cheque. Frydenson's strategy seemed to have worked. I can still see those poor elderly people trooping out of his office, utterly dumbfounded by their summary dismissal. I hope they were satisfied, at least, to have got something for their efforts.

We'd been well represented by Henry. He's a bright guy. Very aggressive. It had been disturbing and exciting, sobering and profitable. I'd earned a lot, and learned a lot.

House clearances! Lawyers! You've got to love them.

10

Stop! Thief!

London Evening Standard
27 September 2011

HANDYMAN WHO STOLE RARE BOOKS
IS JAILED FOR 30 MONTHS

A book thief who stole £36,000 of rare manuscripts, including signed works by Winston Churchill, James Joyce and TS Eliot, has been jailed for two-and-a-half years.

The thief told police he was tempted by the valuable manuscripts and decided to steal them, along with a laptop and £100 in cash. The owners noticed the theft when they returned to their flat at the shop.

Charming, well-educated and articulate, our window-cleaner was agreeable to talk with over a coffee, once the windows were finished. So it seemed reasonable to ask him if he might do a couple of days' work in the house over a weekend: paint the floorboards on the ground floor, and do all the windows inside and out. We gave him the keys and payment in advance, and left for our house in the New Forest.

When we got back on Monday morning, the floorboards were looking pretty good, the windows gleamed. It was only when I sat at my desk that I noticed that my computer was missing. My file of valuable manuscripts and letters was gone, too. A quick look round the house confirmed the further loss of three sweaters, some socks and (unaccountably) some of my underpants. According to a curtain-twitcher across the mews, during his working weekend at our house, the window-cleaner also entertained one, or it may have been several, ladies of the night. I like to think it was his own underpants that he shed.

The loss of the computer was dreadful, as I hadn't backed it up properly, and it contained a novel that I had written some years before, as well as data from my bookselling business that was irreplaceable. The missing plastic folders held autograph letters by a wide variety of major writers, that (individually priced) added up to a total of £36,000. My insurance brokers sent round a loss adjuster, and within a couple of weeks my claim was validated, and I was informed that they would shortly send me a cheque for the full retail price of the lost items. I would happily have sold them all for half that – which would have recovered their initial costs – just to get shot of them.

The day before the settlement was due, an exultant policewoman rang to tell me she had great news! 'The perpetrator has given himself up, and returned the file with your letters in it. He said he felt so badly.' Not as badly as me. I'd have been thrilled to get my computer back – he'd sold that for £100. As for the returned letters? Many of them had been showcased in a variety of my catalogues over the years, and most had been offered at multiple book fairs. Many had been listed on AbeBooks, a website which has been, to my mind, the near ruination of the rare book trade.

Hardly anyone buys individual literary letters. Few private collectors, and – contrary to what you might think – no libraries. You might sell a cache of important letters to an institution, particularly if they are unpublished, but single letters, no matter how fine the content, are near impossible to place in libraries. I'd stocked such material for over twenty years, largely because I quite enjoyed owning it, but there was little profit in it. It was part of what other dealers call inventory, which I regard as stuff I cannot sell. Looked at thus dispassionately, material on a dealer's shelves is an inert form of money, and unless it generates real money, it won't generate more stuff.

When you have as disturbing an experience as this theft, you have to shake yourself, re-confirm your health and happiness and that of your loved ones, and get on with it. And, if this doesn't sound unrealistic, try to learn something. And I did. Not the obvious things: I still don't back up my computers properly, and am increasingly inclined to rely on the kindness of strangers, but what I (at last) understood was that dealing in literary letters is profitless and irritating, and that I should give it up. It was an immense pleasure to buy such material – DH Lawrence writing gossipy letters to his sister-in-law; James Joyce always wanting something; Oscar Wilde trying to be witty; TS Eliot, grudging and precise – they made for company in my office, and I felt subliminally enlarged by them. But the pleasure of their company waned as the years went by, and the letters sat mute and desolate in their leather files, and I similarly in my leather chair. It was time to move on.

I did. A relief, but not that big a deal. But this decision exacerbated and foregrounded another emerging problem in my business, a more dangerous one. 'Existential' is the word now used for this, though I deplore its appropriation from the world of Parisian salons. But in its contemporary meaning – relating to the viability of an enterprise – it fit: not only was I giving up literary letters, which were interesting but hard to sell, I was increasingly bored with books, which were easier to sell but less interesting.

I'd seen the problem coming. From the very start of my business, I had tried to locate and to catalogue the best copies of the best English and American books produced since 1860. For over thirty years I had done that, and seen a great many wonderful things. But it can pall. I'd handled over thirty first editions of *Ulysses*, and twenty of *The Waste Land*, had through my hands some of the virtually unobtainable rarities, obscure first books like Yeats' *Mosada* (1886) and Ezra Pound's *A Lume Spento* (1908). If I dreamt of further, barely unobtainable treasures, the dragons had relinquished their hoards, there was hardly anything left to dream of and to covet. Hardly enough treasure to be worth hunting.

If you sell used books for a living – however fancy and expensive – after a time you will have seen them all, and the next copy is merely an iteration of the previous. Tropical fish sellers will feel similarly about their colourful wares, however exotic. I tried to protect myself from creeping ennui by specialising in books with good inscriptions, annotations, or unusual provenance – books that tell stories – but even that was starting to pall. My usual lassitude was morphing into paralysis. Finding great books was supposed to be hard, heroic even, and increasingly it was becoming easy. I blame the Internet for this.

I began this chapter with a disparaging remark about the website AbeBooks, which lists multiple copies of more than 120 million used books for sale across the world, and on which the great majority of rare and second-hand booksellers are abjectly dependent. I no longer post books for sale on AbeBooks. I dislike it intensely. Let me explain this hardening of my bookseller's arteries, and also – I suppose further explanation is due – why I regard this ubiquitous website as the 'near ruination' of the rare book trade, when it so palpably seems just the opposite.

My reservations about the Internet rare book market are similar to those I have about amazon.com, the Books section of which has supplanted the pleasure of visiting actual bookshops. And yes, it's very efficient. And yes, I use it. In case you didn't know, AbeBooks is owned by Amazon. They smell similar: of oil and steel, cold draughts, and the miserable secretions of an underpaid and overworked staff.

When I began trading in first editions, I made regular scouting trips, often in the company of other dealers. We drove through the countryside visiting local bookshops – every market town had at least one, cities had many – stopping at promising pubs for lunch and a pint, often making detours to see a National Trust property or local museum. At the end of a few days, we would have a box or two of new stock, and a lot of happy memories.

Now, because everyone's stock is online, there are hardly any second-hand and antiquarian bookshops left to visit, partly due to the Internet, but also (sadly) because of the spread of Oxfam Bookshops throughout England. When one of these opens in a village or small town, with its peppercorn rent, free staffing and donated books, within two years the local second-hand bookshop will have closed.

But my dislike of AbeBooks is not merely because it has supplanted a greatly preferable form of life, but because it is full of fake news, fake views, charlatans, incompetents and hucksters. There are few rules, and even they are not enforced. There are no agreed and applicable standards. Second-hand and antiquarian bookselling is not a profession: there are no courses that lead to formal qualifications, no universal testing of competence, no process of certification. Though there are organisations that require signs of competence (in the UK, the Antiquarian Booksellers Association, to which one has to be accepted, and internationally the ILAB), 99.99 per cent of online booksellers belong to no such bodies. It's a free-for-all, a circus, a rodeo, a jungle, a mess. Any damn fool can post books on AbeBooks, and many of them do.

Some examples of what I mean are palpably called for. Let me take them from what I can find today, as I write.

First: let's revert to Chapter 1, in which I went hunting for DH Lawrence first editions after inserting Anna's morning pickle. I'd collected DHL for a few years, and though I searched local bookshops and received the few booksellers' catalogues that were available, I only had a shelf full of books.

That was all I'd been able to find and to afford. So when I discovered that Brooklyn dealer with a plethora of inexpensive Lawrence firsts, it was a shock and a delight. Over the next years, I continued to build on this happy discovery, until I put together a collection of some 160 items.

Now. Today. Let us suppose I want to start building such a collection, and let us rightly suppose, too, that I am languorously desk-bound. I go into AbeBooks and Advance Search under DH Lawrence first editions. Which title shall I look for? Let's start with his (previously) uncommon third novel, *Sons and Lovers*, first edition, published by Duckworth in 1913. Eleven copies, from which one can learn a lot, aside from the obvious fact that if you want one, you can have it, now. The cheapest of these is described as 'very good' – but it has a library stamp, a bookplate, a date stamp on front and rear endpapers, a small tear to the cloth and a 'botched tape reinforcement of the gutter of pages 16–17, else a solid first state copy'. Everything hangs on the else, though buyers unpractised in biblioscepticism will not notice the implications. The copy is scrupulously described (including bibliographic detail) but at the price of $420 should be avoided.

And it has been. It is one of the countless frustrations of the Internet book world that dealers are constantly being told by people with something to sell that 'there is one on the Net' at a certain price, and then trying to sell you their copy – often in inferior condition – at exactly that price. When you remark (1) that the fact that it is on the Net it means it is unsold, and (2) that there is a difference between wholesale and retail, you are greeted by a silence at the other end of the phone, a harrumph, or – which is rather better – the person hangs up.

This provides yet another example of Gekoski's Paradox: the more information a collector has available about the rare book world, the less likely they are to make good decisions. Because you need more than information, you need to know how to interrogate it.

Ten more copies. Let me segue from the cheapest to the most expensive (at $2,750):

> *Fine. 1st Edition. First Edition, First Printing SIGNED by DH Lawrence on a laid in signature. A beautiful book that is in excellent condition. The binding is tight, and the boards are crisp with slight wear to the edges. The pages are exceptionally clean with no writing, marks or bookplates in the book. Overall, a sharp copy of this TRUE FIRST EDITION.*

It's hard to know where to begin. There are four different iterations of the condition of the book: first, it is 'fine'; then 'beautiful'; then there is 'slight wear to the edges'; then it is 'sharp'. These are different. In recent years, the description 'fine', which used to mean without observable defect, now attracts any number of qualifiers – 'very', 'extremely', 'remarkably' – as well as new categories which are presumably better than 'fine': 'gorgeous', 'as new'. I have an American customer who asks, when I offer him what I call a 'fine' copy of a book (which means that it is), 'Is it the best copy in the world?' That is a category that even an extensive search on AbeBooks fails to locate. Who could tell such a thing, except God, whose collection only had the one book, which he gave away.

But I have bigger nits to pick. This copy of *Sons and Lovers* is cunningly misdescribed as 'Signed'; it looks that way on the

Internet, and it actually says 'First printing SIGNED by DH Lawrence . . .' before continuing 'on a laid in signature'. That is, the book is not signed by DH Lawrence. The dealer has clipped a Lawrence signature from a card or letter or minor signed first edition, and 'laid it in'. Is there an attempt to deceive? I will leave that to you to decide. But there are a great many dealers who catalogue books that are not actually signed under the 'SIGNED' category, with clipped signatures or pasted in signed bookplates, and they should desist. The 'professional' booksellers associations have actually written to a number of guilty dealers pointing this out, and suggesting that they abandon the practice in favour of something more . . . accurate. Transparent. And I would add: *honest*. Few of the booksellers contacted agreed to do this, and the booksellers' associations are toothless in this regard. Nor will AbeBooks amend their misleading descriptive practices.

And then we have the non-bibliographic description 'TRUE FIRST EDITION'. Even the modest, cheapest (not) very good copy I cited earlier is quite explicit about which one of the three variants of the first edition theirs is, citing Roberts' Bibliography of DH Lawrence. (Actually there are three further variants. Not a lot of people know this, and certainly Abe's most expensive bookseller wouldn't give a damn.) Theirs is TRUE, a category more appropriate to religion than to first editions.

All this makes me feel like one of Beckett's characters: gloomy, garrulous and inconsolable. 'You go online. I can't go online . . . I will go online,' as the narrator of *The Unnameable* almost mutters. I suspect he was an elderly bookseller, closing shop but not mouth.

How do these fake news booksellers make a living? And if their customers are ignorant, and wish to be ushered from the darkness into the light, how can they do so without adequate guidance? Because AbeBooks cannot provide that: it can be useful if you are already knowledgeable, but if you are not, and are incapable of interrogating the plethora of varied and conflicting information, you will only get more confused, and frequently bilked.

How does one determine the value of a book? In the days before the Internet this was already an interesting conundrum, and dealers had varying opinions about how much a book was worth when buying for stock – that is, whether you could purchase it at x and sell it for more than x. This is partly dependent, of course, on whether you have a good customer base. At a New York Antiquarian Book Fair in the late 1980s, a copy of TS Eliot's *The Waste Land* (Hogarth Press, 1923, one of 460 copies) appeared at a dealer's booth at $12,500. He had bought it some months before from Pierre Berès, a distinguished member of the Paris book trade. It bore a contemporary inscription from the author: '*au grande poète français Paul Valéry homages de l'auteur T.S. Eliot i.xi.23*'. Eliot inscriptions are almost always terse, and this one was (relatively speaking) gushy. In the hours while we dealers were setting up our booths, it sold four more times, from major dealer to major dealer, at nice mark-ups. I eventually purchased it at $24,000, and sold it that evening on the phone for £30,000. The next morning, the dealer from whom I'd bought it the previous day asked if he could buy it back, as it was 'better than I'd first realised'.

The point of this story is that rare books do not have a value, but a range of possible values. (The private owner of the book later sold it at Christie's in 2002 for $101,575). This flexibility of value once led New York's Glenn Horowitz, the most successful contemporary dealer in modern literary books and manuscripts, to claim that the value of a book is 'transactional': it is worth what you can get a buyer to pay for it. When he said this at a conference we were both attending at the University of Texas, I asked him whether, if I could get a multi-millionaire drunk and sell him a book at a ludicrous multiple of what any other copy had ever fetched, that was what the book was worth? The next copy on the market wouldn't be. Yes, he said, that is what it was worth, then and there, in that particular exchange.

'On the day' is a slippery criterion, and open to misuse: a tautology masquerading as a theory, because it is unfalsifiable. Inquiring what a book's fair market value is, is less problematic, if still open to discussion, and subjective within a range, but it depends on citation of prices of other examples of the book. Admittedly, there are no other copies of *The Waste Land* inscribed to Valéry, but I've bought and sold three or four other contemporary inscribed copies (including one to Wyndham Lewis), and they serve as comparables. As a dealer, you have to justify your prices. You can't just make up any damn fat price and hope for the right 'transaction'.

Oh, can't you? Let's hop back to AbeBooks, to see what can be learnt about how to value, and to price, books, because as markets go, it's unregulated and wild. Very *caveat emptor*. I can, as I have said, accept that a book can have a very elastic range of value, from the kinds of bargains I bought all those years ago in Brooklyn, to the extremely high prices some dealers charge on the Internet. But after extremely high, you find extortionate.

Instead of casting about randomly, let me start where I am just now, cataloguing the archive of the late philosopher, man of letters and broadcaster, Brian Magee. Needing to know more about him, I searched for a few of his books, and was offered his *Karl Popper,* published by Collins in the Fontana Modern Masters series, in 1973, and found this copy for sale: 'ISBN 10: 0006329934 ISBN 13: 9780006329930. New Softcover. £2,541.94. From: Irish Booksellers (Portland, ME, USA) Seller Rating: 5-star rating.'

Is this some sort of mistake, either human or algorithmic? I wrote the dealer an innocent email asking if the price was correct, and received no answer. I presume that if I had ordered it, I would have been charged the advertised price.

More information about this seller is easily found. They have numerous books online at these ludicrous prices, perhaps on the supposition that for every thousand people who see them, one wealthy drunken ignoramus might actually transact a purchase. Many complaints have been made about this firm, but AbeBooks takes no responsibility for their offerings. After all, they might say, this seller has a top rating! Five stars! (It is easy to manipulate their rating system.) But if you google 'Irish Booksellers Maine', another set of reviews turns up with 237 entries, all of them giving one star rather than five. One reviewer concludes 'hopefully, AbeBooks will eventually take decisive action & close [them] down'.

Prices on the Internet are interactive: one entry affects others. The Irish Booksellers price on the *Popper* book has a copycat at a less villainous level in Denver, Colorado, priced at £963. (After that, there are eleven copies, rightly priced between £5–£30). I wonder if Mr Horowitz might have trouble with examples like these, even if some dope bought one of the books?

At a lower level of what I regard as questionable practice are the dealers – and there are a lot of them these days – who value 'flat signed' books (which merely have the author's signature) over genuine presentation copies gifted by the author, and charge more for them. Their argument is that a (merely) signed book is better than one presented to any Tom, Dick or Harry who has asked the author to write a personal inscription.

Some authors can be quite canny when asked to inscribe a book, and dismissive: when TS Eliot wrote 'Inscribed for ...' it was a clear signal that he did not know the recipient and had not gifted the book. Anthony Powell could be similarly curt: I once bought from Alan Ross, whom Powell knew well, a couple of books inscribed: 'Alan Ross is hereby confirmed in possession of this book.' Ouch. It happened to me once, when Joseph Heller inscribed a first edition of *Catch 22* to me by writing: 'I hope this book is worth what you paid for it.'

This modern development in favour of 'flat signed' (a horrible term) books has militated against the premium right-fully put on books with a significant association between author and recipient. I recently sold a fine copy of Kazuo Ishiguro's first book, *A Pale View of Hills*, with a warm contemporary inscription from Ishiguro to his friend, the writer Clive Sinclair. If you go on the Net to see other copies of this title, and of other Ishiguro books, very few of them are genuine presentation copies, but there are dozens of books merely bearing the author's signature, carrying inflated prices.

How did this come about? Through a mixture of greed (the dealers) and goodwill (the writer). At book festivals you will inevitably find a long queue of admiring readers who want Ishiguro's latest book signed, sometimes to them, sometimes not. In this queue will be numerous dealers with bags of Ishiguro first editions, asking for a signature on all of them, which the remarkably forbearing and generous Ishiguro supplies, even when the dealer hasn't the courtesy to buy the newly released title. These signed copies soon find their way on to AbeBooks, valuing the new signature at between £200 and £1,000, depending on which book it is on.

Well, at least these are first editions, a term that means the very first printing of the book, and which is what collectors used to insist upon. But as prices of rare books rose, and the value of dust wrappers skyrocketed, a new market was created selling later printings, often delineated as 'impressions'. Slowly, collectors who could not afford a decent copy of a valued first edition began to be offered, and to buy, a 'first edition, second (third, fourth . . .) impression'. Thus we have an Abe entry for Ishiguro's: '*The Remains of the Day*, Faber & Faber, 1989. Hardcover. Condition: Very Good. Dust Jacket Condition: Very Good. Faber & Faber, 1989. This is a First Edition Second Impression in very good condition. £60.'

You can buy a genuine first, in better condition, for twice that. Do it! When I started dealing, there was no premium attached to later impressions, which were rightly regarded as reprints, and had value only as second-hand books. After all, the first edition is printed first, later impressions are printed later. The implication to my mind is that if you cannot afford a genuine first in a wrapper, buy it without one – at least it is real.

You will understand by now why the pleasure and excitement of selling first editions was beginning to pall, and why I was doing less and less of it. But if I gave up dealing in books as well as letters, what was left? Still call yourself a bookseller, do you? Presumably, as in: 'retired'? Which I did not wish to be. I enjoy the world of first editions and antiquarian books, have made dozens of warm relationships with members of the trade, writers, book collectors, and librarians, and know how quickly these friendships fade when you exit the form of life which generates and supports them.

There was, then, only one thing left to do to develop my business, and fortunately it was an area in which I had some experience: cataloguing and selling writers' and publishers' archives, to me a much more interesting and worthy area of the rare book trade. Do more of that!

Archives? Let's start at the beginning. An archive consists of the mass of personal papers that fill a writer's study, closets, floors and attic, and (if you ask their partner) most of the rest of the house. The terminal moraine of an author's life. What is to be found there? Well, in ideal state – with, as Gertrude Stein put it, with 'no pieces of paper thrown away' – you might find: the author's manuscripts and drafts of work both published and unpublished; diaries or journals; incoming correspondence, and (if you are very lucky) copies of the author's outgoing letters as well; historical material that documents the author's life, like photographs and family memorabilia; and objects of significance: such as the writer's desk, typewriter or computer, or (even) best Sunday suit. Not underpants. This material will have spread like an infestation through the house, and found nesting places in boxes and cartons, filing cabinets, bookshelves, and drawers both open and private ('No one is looking into my drawers!' William Golding once warned me).

I have spent a lot of time in attics, studies, and cellars, sifting through myriad unsorted boxes and cartons of a writer's stuff – dust! damp! – and there is something dirty and invasive about the process that makes you both literally and figuratively need a wash. When, eventually, you have carted all the stuff away, it then has to be catalogued. This is a rough and approximate process: even in the 20–50 pages of one of my descriptive archive catalogues, most of the material is left out. There's too much.

Though a putative purchaser may come for a day or two to look through the material, there is no way anyone can account for every item. The eventual purchase has to be in good faith. Generally, it's worth it, and after an archive is sold to an institution, wonderful and unexpected items may pop up. When it is put on display or exhibition, an archive bursts into life. It is, after all, on the basis of such collections of assiduously preserved pieces of paper that we come to have accurate recordings of ourselves and others: biographies get written, journals are published, *Collected Works and Letters* come into print, history is made.

But, and this is sad news for the vast majority of writers, most archives are of no financial value, though they are, of course, of interest to the writer's family and friends. Libraries only want archives of well-known writers and publishers whose material will be extensively consulted by researchers. American librarians sometimes ask: 'How many books, articles and PhDs can come out of this?'

I've had the privilege of selling the archives of writers such as Peter Ackroyd, Angela Carter, Rachel Cusk, John Fowles, Geoffrey Hill, Kazuo Ishiguro, Penelope Lively, and many others, as well as the publishers Victor Gollancz, André Deutsch, *Granta* magazine, and Weidenfeld & Nicolson. When this works, it's great. On the other hand, I have sometimes wasted weeks cataloguing and researching an archive, only to find that I cannot locate a buyer. Or that the owner has withdrawn the commission, and then sold it themselves, or through another dealer.

But there are worse problems. It can be hard to assess the importance of an archive. I once made the mistake of telling Sue Townsend, whose *Adrian Mole* books I adore, that there would be no market for her papers, as it is only 'literary' archives that draw researchers in sufficient numbers. Her papers are now, quite rightly, in the University of Leicester Library, and I'll bet they are consulted regularly. You learn more about contemporary English social history from Sue Townsend than from a basketful of social scientists.

So after my Theft in the Mews learning experience, the readjustment of my dealing life produced a new and better balance. I usually have ten or so authors' archives on the go – a process made much more difficult by Covid, because many libraries have closed, and on reopening will need their diminished budgets just to pay the staff and to meet recurrent expenses. A hard time to place an archive, though since the pandemic began I've sold four, which I reckon is pretty good.

In that time, I've only sold a couple of dozen books, mostly bought especially for particular customers. But I'm still looking. I will always buy an interesting book, at the right price. Why wouldn't I? It's what I do.

11

Get Me Out of Here! The Publishing Archive of Victor Gollancz

One morning I had a phone call from Malcolm Edwards, the Publishing Director of Orion Books, inquiring in gentle tones whether I might care to discuss a 'possible project'. I didn't ask of what sort, just put on a jacket and headed his way. When you've been in the trade as long as I, you can smell it when something interesting is about to happen. Though even a nose as large and as sophisticated as mine wouldn't have supposed the project – which should certainly have been called 'projects' – would take eight years. It took Joyce less time than that to write *Ulysses*. I have never encountered anything as vast and as daunting as what was to come.

Malcolm had the sense to lead me gently into the arena – think gladiators – in a series of steps, without revealing the full extent of what was to come. Julius Caesar knew this, too. First you release a mangy lion, but you hold the really fearsome stuff for later. All that was required, Malcolm told me, was getting rid of a bunch of second-hand books, on behalf of Orion, who were planning ahead: their warehouse,

Littlehampton Book Services in Sussex, was going to close in 2018. It was home to millions of new books, but also 'a lot' of old ones, which had to go. No one on the Orion Board cared where they went, or to whom; Malcolm was simply charged with monetising them as best he could. Could I, he inquired mildly but with something of a glint in his eye, manage to dispose of them on behalf of Orion?

'Certainly,' I said, 'lead me to them!'

My first visit to the warehouse was on a freezing, grey winter morning in 2012, with an amused Malcolm at my side. We entered through an unassuming door, signed in at the modest reception desk, and soon entered the shelved space. It was enormous, bigger than multiple football grounds. It was cold, it was draughty, it was hideous. Impossible to enter without a shudder, and a frisson, not mild, of anxiety, Littlehampton Book Services (LBS) served as a distribution warehouse for a considerable number of major book publishers, whose volumes were stacked on acres of iron shelves that rose 40ft in the air, and were constantly filled and emptied by men driving forklifts, raising and lowering pallets of books. You had to don a bright orange vest to enter the space, and stay carefully within the yellow pedestrian walkways, else you might be scooped up on to a shelf; mordant rumours abounded of skeletons found on the top shelves of some of the less visited areas of the warehouse.

Next to the toilets on the ground floor, an iron staircase rose some fifty precarious steps to an upper floor, and a very different, if equally daunting, scene. Under a lower ceiling ranged aisle after aisle of iron bookshelves, containing the retained file copies (usually examples of the first edition) of a variety of publishers including Cassells, JM Dent, Weidenfeld & Nicolson, Ward Lock, Ernest Benn, and pre-eminently Victor Gollancz, 15,000 of whose books were stuffed on to the shelves.

Not a lot of people knew this, of course. You couldn't just knock on the door of the LBS, announce you were rather keen on file copies, and ask for a quick look round. You had to have an introduction, then sign in, then be issued a pass, then put on your jacket, then be escorted to whatever area you wished to visit. It's probably easier to break into the Royal Mint, or Broadmoor. I have no idea why they were quite so protective: had they imagined hordes of pathological biblio-philes slavering to ransack the premises? Quite the opposite. I never saw anyone there except the many employees, who always looked at me inquisitively. They had to be there – why would I wish to? And the reason was simple – or appeared simple at the outset – and that was the magic of the very name 'Gollancz'.

Victor Gollancz Ltd is one of the most important English publishing firms of the twentieth century. Founded in 1927, it has published books of the highest quality over a uniquely wide range, which created a complex set of problems when I had to sort and to sell (at the highest possible price) all of the retained books. Or almost all. There is a rule that infallibly pertains when you examine a publishing house's file copies: the more valuable the book, the less likely it is still to be there. In the case of the Gollancz books, this theorem proved perfectly accurate.

A few words by way of background are necessary here. After he graduated from Oxford, Gollancz worked for six years for the firm of Ernest Benn, quickly establishing himself as so intelligent, so driven, and so creatively engaged with the business of publishing, that he was soon offered a partnership in the business. But growing disagreements with the conservative Benn were inevitable, and young Victor had no trouble raising substantial money to start his own imprint. He was universally recognised as a rising star: within eight months he had already paid a dividend of 7½ per cent to his investors. The *Daily News* noted that his firm 'had broken every precedent, and nearly every record', and the Chairman of Heinemann, Charles Evans, wrote to congratulate the newcomer: 'You are a rival worthy of one's esteem.'

In the first years, Gollancz signed the young George Orwell, published the wildly successful detective novels of Dorothy Sayers, promoted Daphne du Maurier and AJ Cronin, and used the profits to finance the establishment of the Left Book Club, a string of orange paperbacks devoted to socialism, pacifism, penal reform, child welfare and other pressing social issues.

When the firm was founded, Gollancz wanted to make an immediate splash. He had a genius for branding (as it was not yet called), and set out to establish an exciting and varied list of books, and to make them instantly recognisable. Thus many of his earliest titles had magnificent art deco dust wrappers by the great graphic artist Edward McKnight Kauffer. But even these – wonderful though they were – were not sufficiently eye-catching. In 1929 Gollancz books began to appear – as they would for the next forty years – in bright yellow wrappers with blocky typefaces in either black or magenta. They recalled the 'yellowbacks' sold at railway stalls in the last decades of the nineteenth century, but these were books of higher quality and even greater visibility. They could be recognised from 50ft away.

This marketing coup was accompanied by an equivalent advertising innovation. From the earliest years, Gollancz spent an enormous amount buying space in the major papers and magazines, and, again, the offerings were instantly recognisable. In large black typeface, the adverts were personal, immediate, provocative ... and hugely successful. Other publishers sniffed their disapproval at the young upstart, but there was no doubt about it: in the early 1930s Gollancz was the brightest, most aggressive and innovative of English publishers. Profitable as well: in no time further substantial dividends were being paid to investors, and as the books rolled out, new authors were banging at the door begging to be let in, many recognising that Gollancz was the right publisher for a writer with a message.

It was unprecedented for a major commercial publisher – which within ten years Gollancz certainly was – also to be a politically engaged and crusading one. He was committed to publishing significant books at low prices 'designed to convert people on a big scale to socialism and pacifism'. The Left Book Club, run by Victor together with John Strachey and Harold Laski, issued the first of its 'selections' for Club members in 1936, and membership rose precipitously. In May of that year there were 9,000 members, five months later there were 28,000, and figures continued to rise.

The Left Book Club was designed to initiate, to promote, and even to finance a mass political movement. Theatre and reading groups were formed, summer schools created, political candidates were elicited and supported, annual rallies were held in London, millions of pamphlets and leaflets were distributed to raise political awareness. The post-war election of a Labour Government was partly the result of Gollancz's passionate campaigning: 'a genuine movement of the masses', he called it.

A variety of major books, by authors like George Orwell and Arthur Koestler, were included in the 262 volumes eventually published by the Club. During the pre-war years the Left Book Club was what the American historian Stuart Samuels describes as 'the greatest single force in England for the dissemination of left-wing thought'.

And that's not all; sometimes readers needed some respite from all this high-mindedness. Gollancz actively championed high-quality detective fiction, which was not only a source of great income, but of great pride, within the firm. Pre-eminent, of course, was Dorothy L Sayers, but she was joined, in this 'golden age' of detective fiction, by Michael Innes, Gladys Mitchell, Edmund Crispin, Phoebe Atwood Taylor, John Franklin Bardin, and Ellery Queen.

Queen, who joined Gollancz as early as 1929, was of course an American author. His highly successful sales, and Gollancz's interest in America and American writing, provided the impetus for Victor's energetic attempt to introduce more American writers to his list. Some of the major figures were already published in England – Fitzgerald, Faulkner, Frost, Hemingway, Sinclair Lewis – but unless an American was already a bestseller in the home market, no English publisher would sign them.

Victor began to make regular, frenetic trips to New York, and was never happy unless he came back with at least twenty new books. Indeed, by 1951, half of the new titles issued by Gollancz were by American authors. The list included John Cheever, Ralph Ellison, Edna Ferber, Betty Friedan, John Irving, Archibald MacLeish, Joyce Carol Oates, James Purdy, John Updike, Kurt Vonnegut, Edward Lewis Wallant, and Richard Wright. No other English firm published so many significant Americans.

Nor so many women: unlike his publishing contemporaries, Gollancz actively sought and aggressively promoted female writers. Sayers and Du Maurier were joined in the 1930s lists by Phyllis Bentley, Elizabeth Bowen, Vera Brittain, Ivy Compton-Burnett, Naomi Mitchison, Edith Sitwell, and Dodie Smith, who were all popular, and sold regularly.

This list is swollen when you add the names of some of the greats of science fiction, a genre that Gollancz Publishers didn't so much promote, as actually invent, in the UK. The list included giants of science and fantasy fiction such as Isaac Asimov and Arthur C Clarke, to whom were added further major figures like Samuel R Delany, Philip K Dick, Philip José Farmer, William Gibson, Robert Heinlein, Frank Herbert, Ursula Le Guin, and Walter Miller. (Later English additions included Brian Aldiss, JG Ballard, Terry Pratchett, and Philip Pullman.) Sales in the area of detective and fantasy fiction, since the list began to grow in the 1970s under the editorial stewardship of Malcolm Edwards, have been enormous.

Too many lists? I'm sorry to seem a pedant, but I need to give some idea, however sketchy, of how daunting the coming project was going to be. Most of the first editions by these authors (and thousands more) were stored in that upstairs room at the LBS. As I first perused the contents of the shelves, walking up and down the many 40ft-long aisles, I was doing what I usually do, what I most care about and am best at, and that is seeking the most valuable books, but my eye isn't sharp enough to pick out a £1,000 book when it is surrounded by hundreds of books of lesser or no value. I prefer going into a bookshop and being shown the few most exciting items, while I drink a coffee or a glass of wine, and hope to buy one or two of them. I am the opposite of a book scout, a category of person I admire and but have no desire to emulate. I needed the services of one of them!

One of the most assiduous book scouts in London, the exhaustingly ebullient Adam Blakeney, once told me that on entering an antiquarian bookshop he hadn't been in for some weeks, he could immediately spot the books which had been added to the shelves since his last visit. I didn't believe this, it was inconceivable, and bet him a good lunch he couldn't do it. We went to the well-established and comprehensively stocked Bertram Rota on Long Acre, where we were greeted by the reserved and wary Anthony Rota, who didn't much like either of us, and Adam proved he could indeed do it, pulling book after book from shelf after shelf, and asking the reluctant Anthony if it was new stock? It was, each and every book. Adam had an enormous steak for his victory lunch, with some chips and a Coke. He gets nauseous if he eats a fruit or a vegetable, which has led me to call him both.

It was Adam – by this time employed by Peter Harrington Books – whom I consulted, after I'd recovered sufficiently from my first visit to the warehouse. I inquired of him plaintively, 'What the hell am I supposed to do with all these fucking books?'

Within a few days, dressed up nice and warmly, he visited the LBS with me. Unlike my eyes, which cloud with tears in the presence of too many books, his lit up. Heaven! Within half an hour he had worked out (I almost said located, but I'm not sure if you can locate an absence, I'm only a bookseller not a metaphysician) what *wasn't* there. And that was, predictably, the most valuable books: there were none of the pre-war Orwells in dust jackets; of the du Mauriers, no *Rebecca*; most of the early Dorothy L Sayers were missing; the list went on and on. Curiously enough, however, I knew where the missing Orwells had gone, and had a pretty clear idea of who had stolen them, because some fifteen years before, three beautiful early Orwells in dust jackets, stamped 'FILE COPY' in black ink, were on sale at the June Book Fair of the Provincial Booksellers Fairs Association, from which they were bought by an American dealer and taken for display at the larger and swankier Antiquarian Booksellers Association Fair that was going on concurrently, who sold them to yet another American bookseller for yet another profit.

Adam knew this, too; it was common enough knowledge in the trade, and most of us felt we could pinpoint the ex-Gollancz employee who had pilfered them. I informed Malcolm of this useful fact, and was surprised that he didn't care. Years had passed, you couldn't prove anything, why waste time thinking about it? Adam and I were impressed by his sang-froid, and resolved never to tell the story again, until we had a good opportunity.

'OK, Adam,' I said wearily, as we finished our first three-hour tour of the shelves, 'what do we do now?'

'Categories!' he said. 'You have to break them up and find the right buyer for the right books.' That is, it was like a house clearance, only multiplied by a thousand.

'Tell me about it!' I said, meaning, that's for sure, what a nightmare! But he took me literally, and started issuing instructions.

'Let's start with Gollancz: you might find a buyer ...' – he looked up and raised his eyebrows in a *that would be me* fashion – 'for all of the pre-war books. That's where to start. Then hive off the residual detective fiction and the science fiction, then the American authors, and then find individual books that can be sold separately, and then get rid of the rump. I can tell you who to approach: you'll need to offer each section to at least two dealers.'

It wasn't as easy as that, though it was a start. Every couple of weeks, Adam and Malcolm and I visited the warehouse, often accompanied by my associate Peter Grogan, whose role was to increase as the project expanded. Within a few months Adam's firm of Harrington's had purchased the pre-war Gollancz copies, having bid twice as much as the perfectly reputable under-bidder. But Adam was not going to let these books go to anyone else, he loved every yellow-bellied one of them.

As the months passed, the job expanded and the tens of thousands of non-Gollancz books began to get sorted and categorised, and possible buyers came to view the material, most of whom shrugged and went home to a soothing cup of Bovril. By the time three or perhaps four years had passed, we were down to the lumpen proletariat: still many thousands of books that were neither part of an essential category nor valuable in themselves. What to do?

First, charitably, Malcolm suggested Oxfam. A long phone call with one of their book buyers established that they didn't think it worth a visit. It was then that I learnt that, in the used book market, as opposed to the rare book one, the most undesirable and least valuable books are hardback fiction. Novels look nice on the shelves, one dealer told us, but that is where they stay, until the day you try to give them away, and find no one will take them.

Our last call was to the enormously enterprising Nigel Burwood, whose Charing Cross bookshop, Any Amount of Books, is generally true to its name. Undaunted by quantity, Nigel knew how to make a profit which factors in the huge costs of shipping, shelving, and cataloguing tens of thousands of books. Even he didn't wish to visit, but after various entreaties, he sent one of his employees, who offered less than twenty pence a book. We took it gratefully. Within a month the warehouse shelves were almost bare, a few obscure books hanging on for dear life, though round the perimeter were dozens of filing cabinets housing the publishing files of JM Dent and Weidenfeld & Nicolson, to which we would have to return.

Most of the books disposed of, there was scant time for recuperation, much less self-congratulation. Because selling those tens of thousands of variegated, dusty and unsorted volumes, glimmering in the penumbral neon light, that was easy in comparison to the trials to come. If you ventured further into the depths of that warehouse, at once a hellhole and a lunatic bibliophiles' paradise, at the end of a corridor so long, and with so many twists, turns and doors, that I got lost every time I tried to find my way either in or out, and had to telephone for help, you eventually came to a windowless room at the end of the building, where you would find yet more filing cabinets. Dozens and dozens of them, old, rusty and dusty, stuffed with all of the production, editorial, and rights files of Gollancz Publishers, the vast majority unopened for perhaps fifty years. They had an abandoned look: many of the drawers would no longer open, and those that did were stuffed so tightly with files that it was hard to extract any single one. Nor could one tell which to choose, for most of them had lost the little plastic namey-thingy at the top that indicated what they contained. No principle of organisation was evident: alphabetical order, if it once pertained, had been ruthlessly displaced. Loads of files for loads of books: good luck finding anything you were looking for specifically.

The archive was contained in fifty cabinets of four drawers each, the great majority of which contained the individual files for the books published by Victor Gollancz up to the date 2000. These were a source of unending frustration and fascination, promising more than they willingly delivered. They characteristically contained: (1) letters between the author and/or his agent with the publishers, regarding commissioning of the book, and its production; (2) contracts for initial purchase of the book, and for any further editions and transfers of rights; (3) reader's reports, often from the redoubtable Jon Evans, whose input was the firm's major editorial response to a manuscript; (4) letters to the author, tens of thousands of them, frequently from Gollancz himself, generally of length and substance; and (5) the author's replies. Alas, Gollancz didn't retain their memorable design and marketing files, and the material regarding the political and social activities of the Left Book Club has been lost.

The most obvious attractions of the archive lie in the correspondence from the major authors, and there are significant numbers of fascinating letters from authors such as Kingsley Amis, Daphne du Maurier, George Orwell, Dorothy L Sayers, George Bernard Shaw and John Updike, amongst many others. From these files, we learnt that unlike many publishers of the time, Gollancz did not submit an author's manuscript to an editorial process of revision. It was an in-house matter of principle that writers should be entirely in control of their own texts. As Victor put it: 'After all, this editing business is comparatively new, and it is only applicable to prose ... Imagine a music publisher "editing" a composer's work! Or an art dealer insisting on an artist modifying a painting! ... If I were an author I would sooner (or very nearly) starve than let anyone hack my book about.'

It's hard not to feel reflexively sympathetic, and to begin to ponder what the differences are, after all, between a symphony, a painting, and a novel, such that only the latter requires editorial input. Gollancz books were merely copy-edited, and then only with the consent of the author: Daphne du Maurier was a bad punctuator, and happy to be moulded into shape, whereas Edna Ferber, who had a passionate dislike of commas, insisted her work be printed exactly as submitted. In each case it was the author's wish that prevailed.

You can imagine what Gollancz was objecting to when you recall the words of the legendary American editor, Maxwell Perkins, who famously enjoined his writers (who included Fitzgerald, Hemingway, and Wolfe): 'Just get it down on paper, and then we'll see what to do with it.' The 'we' here sounds a little too collaborative, and perhaps admonitory. But, in fact, Perkins' final position – 'I believe the writer ... should always be the final judge. I have always held to that position and have sometimes seen books hurt thereby, but at least as often helped. The book belongs to the author ...' – is not dissimilar to that of Gollancz himself.

And what a lot of books Gollancz issued! Some famously memorable, but 95 per cent of them justly forgotten. The most exciting archival material of course, was the letters written by the most famous writers, which emerged slowly from their filing cabinets, and were often greeted by spasms and shrieks of delight. Over a couple of years, Peter Grogan began to put together an overall description of the archive, in order to offer it to potential buyers. After each trip to the warehouse – I am incompetent to do the kind of coalface foraging that he is so good at – he would return to the office with his discoveries.

Between these it is hard to choose, though number one is indisputable. It is a letter from Eric Blair (George Orwell) to Gollancz sending him a new manuscript to consider for publication. From his very first book (*Down and Out in Paris and London*) Gollancz and Orwell had an amiable working relationship. Orwell's books appealed to the publisher's interests and values, as examples of the best kind of left-wing social realism, and though they never sold all that well (except for *The Road to Wigan Pier*) they were staples of the Gollancz list. And then, on 19 March 1944, Victor received a letter from Orwell, half-heartedly suggesting that the firm publish his new fiction: '... a little fairy story, about 30,000 words, with a political meaning. But I must tell you that it is I think completely unacceptable politically from your point of view (it is anti-Stalin).'

Animal Farm! The author asked his publisher if he wanted to read it, but if not to let him know quickly so that he might try elsewhere. Gollancz's reply, dated 23 March 1944, says that he would certainly like to read the manuscript, and denies that he is toeing the Stalinist line, having opposed Soviet foreign policy before the war.

Orwell's next letter, two days later, reiterates that he does not feel Gollancz will publish it, but will send him the manuscript. Though criticising Stalin from the Left rather than the Right, he notes that 'in my experience this gets one into even worse trouble'. Upon reading the manuscript, Gollancz replied to Orwell, 'You were right and I was wrong. I am so sorry. I have returned the manuscript ...' In an additional letter sent to Orwell's literary agent on the same day, Gollancz responded: 'I am highly critical of many aspects of internal and external Soviet policy: but I could not possibly publish (as Blair anticipated) a general attack of this nature.'

Many other publishers didn't want it either. Faber's TS Eliot demurred, saying that what the text needed was 'more public-spirited pigs', which in the context of his full letter is not quite as silly as it sounds. The manuscript made the rounds, and its author was becoming more and more dejected, when it was purchased by Frederic Warburg, and published the next year to considerable acclaim. And of course, four years later, Warburg had the rights to *Nineteen Eighty-Four*. So poor, upright Victor Gollancz, having supported Orwell in the publications of worthy books unaccompanied by significant sales, missed out on the two bestsellers.

It happened to Victor more than once, indeed it is a staple of publishing history: an author gets started with a small-ish publisher who supports him though sales are meagre, then moves on. Two further instances in Gollancz's stable of authors were John le Carré and John Updike. Victor had been delighted to publish the former's *A Call from the Dead* and *A Murder of Quality*, which sold modestly, and then thrilled to have published *The Spy Who Came in from the Cold*, which was soon reprinted nineteen times. Following which, Gollancz received a letter from le Carré's agent, to inform him that the author was moving to another publisher. Gollancz immediately wrote a series of astonished, then plaintive, then furious letters to his author, which received no reply.

John Updike published two books with Gollancz before leaving: *Hoping for a Hoopoe* and *The Poorhouse Fair* are largely and rightly forgotten these days, but the young writer's next manuscript was more than promising. *Rabbit, Run* immediately captured Gollancz's enthusiastic attention and marked Updike as a writer worth supporting and promoting – but not, Victor was sorry to conclude, by himself. The correspondence between them is heart-rending, and has its funny moments.

On first reading the *Rabbit* manuscript, Victor wrote effusively to Updike. But he was a little puzzled, he had to admit, by a bit of American slang with which he was unfamiliar: what is the meaning of the term 'blow job'? Updike replied, with a bloodlessly crisp definition – 'the mouth–genital contact scientifically named fellatio' – to which the apparently innocent Victor replied that it sounded delightful 'if accompanied by love'. The restrained and elegant Updike did not make the obvious rejoinder. But his publisher, warned by his legal team of the possible repercussions of publishing a sexually explicit novel, decided not to take the risk. The novel was soon published by André Deutsch.

These few instances alone, as they most assuredly were not, provide ample evidence of how fascinating a literary archive can be. After some eighteen months, I was ready to offer the Gollancz papers for sale to a library, rightly maintaining in our sales document that they had 'immense research interest across a wide variety of writers, themes, and topics'. The asking price was £1 million.

Two archivists from the British Library came to have a look, peered and shivered, and returned a few weeks later to have another go. It was obvious what they would say: yes, the papers were of very considerable interest, and certainly should be in the national collections. But – there's so often a but – the question was whether they could raise the money. The Library's annual budget did not allow a purchase from in-house funds, so it would have to apply for national grants. But there would be competing acquisition requests and projects from other departments within the Library, and it would be a question of which to foreground. Gollancz wasn't chosen, and they regretfully decided against pursuing the matter.

My next port of call, as often, was the University of Texas. Tom Staley immediately saw the research value of the material, and was particularly taken by the American authors represented in the archive. The price – now $2 million at the prevailing rate of exchange – seemed reasonable to him.

'Give me a week,' he said. 'We'll know where we are by then.'

This meant that he would pick up his phone(s) and see if he could raise the money from his donors – the Friends of the

Library, Board Members, and associated wealthy patrons – to see who might stump up.

A week later he rang me back.

'You know what?' he said. 'It's the damnedest thing, but since 9/11 I find it almost impossible to raise funds for non-American material . . .'

Good ol' rich Texans, I thought, patriotic to the core, and unlikely to be swayed by the prospect of donating to buy an archive of a socially radical, communist-sympathising publisher.

'Thanks for offering it,' said Tom.

I made a few further inquiries at other universities, but had no luck. What was of interest to all of them, though, were the files pertaining to authors well represented in their own collections. And this meant the inevitable, the dreaded, the protracted, frustrating conclusion: Break It Up!

The archive gave a detailed and compelling picture of a remarkable man, and a unique publishing house. Though it had already been used as research material for books on both Victor and his publishing business, there was still an immense amount to be learnt from it, consulted in its entirety. Normally, one might have counselled patience, assuming that since it was the right stuff, the right buyer would come along in time. I had been asked to present and to represent the material, and if its owners didn't care a hoot how it was sold, I did. It needed to be kept together. But the date for clearing the warehouse was closing in, and the contents of those filing cabinets would have to find, if not a new home, then a lot of new homes. I viewed this not merely as a shame, but as a defeat.

Over the next few years, we undertook the enormous task

of finding those new homes. The hundreds of author files were individually described and catalogued, and dozens of dealers and private customers bought one or another. Over sixty libraries made purchases, including the British Library, the National Libraries of Scotland, Wales, and Ireland, and a host of American institutions. The money rolled in – though less than the £1 million asking price, we got reasonably close to it – but the project felt more and more of a mopping up operation rather than a series of small but discernible triumphs.

I wasn't at the coalface for most of this, which was largely orchestrated by Malcolm and Peter, as I devoted my time increasingly to curating the FEST charity auction for English PEN, and to writing those four of my books which fell within the period. I enjoyed this enormously, and for a time considered giving up my dealing life entirely.

I didn't. I couldn't. For an established book dealer there's no good reason to say goodbye, and no way to either. I kept dealing, I kept writing. Sometimes they get in each other's way, but like most people of a certain age, I've learnt to shuffle along.

12

Defacing My Own Book!

Lord Dalmeny was having a ball. We were in London on 21 May 2013, and the Chair of Sotheby's was at the rostrum for a gala charity auction in aid of English PEN, teasing, bullying, cajoling every last penny out of the audience of collectors, writers, and celebrities who overflowed into the aisles.

'Lot 25,' he said smoothly. 'Thomas Keneally's *Schindler's Ark*. Winner of the Booker Prize, great book, great film. Wonderful annotations by the author! Who'll start me at two thousand pounds?'

The bidding proceeded briskly. Keneally, the most gregarious and generous of men, had filled 137 pages of the first edition with 2,500 words of commentary and reflection about the book, and it was likely to do well. Ion Trewin, Administrator of the Man Booker Prize and formerly the editor of *Schindler's Ark*, was looking on anxiously.

'I'm longing to buy it,' he told me over drinks before the sale began. 'Do you think seven thousand pounds would get it? I can't go further than that.'

'I don't know,' I said cautiously. 'There's never been an

auction like this, and it's extremely hard to guess what the books might fetch. At your usual literary auction there are precedents and comparables, so they can give estimates that will be pretty accurate. But with unique material? Each book a first edition with retrospective annotations by the author? Who knows? That's why there are no estimates printed in the catalogue.'

Lord Dalmeny was pushing along. 'New bidder. Five thousand pounds. Thank you, sir.' He looked round the room. 'Five thousand five hundred pounds ... Six thousand pounds ... Six thousand five hundred pounds ...'

Looking disappointed, Ion put his hand up for the final time.

'Seven thousand pounds ... Seven thousand five hundred pounds ...'

As the bidding spiralled upwards, Lord Dalmeny looked down towards Eric Abraham, the South African film and theatre producer, who had been buying heavily, supporting the cause and building his collection simultaneously. To Abraham's obvious discomfort, Dalmeny had taken to referring to him teasingly as 'Bank of England'.

'Bank of England? Something from you, sir?

'Twelve thousand pounds ... Thirteen thousand pounds ... Fourteen thousand pounds. Are we all done at fourteen thousand pounds? Last chance!'

He looked around the room beseechingly, members of the audience laughed, ducking and wincing. He'd already urged a gentleman buyer to make a more thrusting bid, in case his lady wife, who was at his side, declined her favours later in the evening. The gentleman blushed, smirked and demurred. His wife was not amused.

The gavel came down. It was a price in line with the previous high spots:

- Julian Barnes' first novel *Metroland* (the copy that he originally inscribed to his parents when it was published), made £14,000: '... working title was "No Weather" – because I was going to put absolutely no reference to the weather in it ...' And later: 'Rather too much research showing here – tho' it was I remember a hard passage to write. Make the history of the Metropolitan line a metaphor for what happened to the human soul in suburbia without it showing too much. Not easy.'
- Alan Bennett, *The Uncommon Reader*, £11,000. With 650 words of annotation on 18 pages, and a charming ink self-portrait on the title page.
- Roald Dahl, *Matilda*, £30,000. Quentin Blake extra-illustrated this copy with eight delightful drawings of Matilda reading a book.
- Edmund de Waal, *The Hare with Amber Eyes*, £14,500. The Illustrated Edition, extensively annotated on 39 pages, with tipped-in, handmade white envelopes with inserted contemporary postcards and photographs.
- Seamus Heaney, *Death of a Naturalist*, £17,000. Above the text of the poem 'At a Potato Digging', Heaney wrote: 'Anthony Thwaite once described me (to my face) as "laureate of the root vegetable".'
- Kazuo Ishiguro, *The Remains of the Day*, £18,000. With six full-page ink drawings by the author, illustrating scenes in the book, and 2,050 words of annotation. On a passage describing the rise and fall of butlers: 'Melvyn

Bragg commented in print that this passage was really about the London literary scene. I think he was right!'

And the big one was yet to come.

Not all the books did this well, and not all authors pursued their annotating task with such enthusiasm, but most of the books fetched significant sums. A number of the contributing writers came along on the evening. I could spot Justin Cartwright, Wendy Cope, Howard Jacobson, David Lodge, Lionel Shriver, Colm Tóibín, Joanna Trollope and Jeanette Winterson looking on a trifle anxiously as their books came up for sale. Some did well, others less so, some writers minded, others didn't. Writers have to live with the fact that some (too many!) of their contemporaries get higher advances, more enthusiastic reviews, and bigger sales. So why not higher bids at auction? They are used to the disappointments and humiliations that this can engender, but many never get over them: many writers I know are envious of the success of their fellows. Gore Vidal put this wonderfully: 'It is not enough to succeed, others must fail.' In case you mistake this for a truism – neither can exist without the other – Vidal clarified it unambiguously: 'every time a friend succeeds, I die a little.'

It was universally agreed that FEST, as it came to be called, was on behalf of a great cause. Founded in London in 1921, English PEN has the admirable motto 'Freedom to Read, Freedom to Write', and describes itself thus: 'The founding centre of PEN International, a worldwide writers' association with 145 centres in more than 100 countries . . . We campaign to defend writers and readers in the UK and around the world whose human right to freedom of expression is at risk . . . We work to remove inequalities, where they exist, which prevent people's enjoyment and learning from literature.'

PEN is thus, near as damn it, a union for writers, and as such is widely supported by them, as we had certainly learnt. Its English Board of Trustees consists of writers, editors, translators, publishers and literary journalists. I am none of the above, but a little of a few, which was sufficient to get me elected to that body in 2011. I was flattered by this, but it wasn't long before I realised, and not much longer before the others did, that I was not fit for purpose. I have a general disposition in favour of freedom of expression, and am horrified by the incarceration and harassment of writers round the world, but I'm a terrible committee man.

I found the passion of my new colleagues highly admirable and a little daunting, and sat through Board meetings in a state of semi-consciousness, not having read the many agenda items with sufficient care. I scanned the minutes, matters arising, the reports of Chair and Treasurer, budgets, submissions from the heads of various subcommittees, plans for future projects. Nothing stuck. By the end of my first year of service, I understood that someone else – almost anyone else – could do the job better than I. What to do? Either I could drift on, or stop attending meetings, or resign, which seemed a bit drastic, and embarrassing to have to explain.

And then something totally unexpected happened, and suddenly I was going to be more than useful. One day after yet another interminable Board meeting, our Chair Jonathan Heawood asked me if we could have a coffee, as he had a project in mind.

I may be bad at meetings, but I'm great at coffee.

'Sure, of course! What's it all about?'

'Well,' he said, 'a few years ago your agent Peter Straus had one of his good ideas, and suggested that PEN, which is (as you now know) always short of funds, might raise some money at a charity auction ...'

My heart sank. Charity auctions are a bore, and unless they involve myriad wealthy and well-lubricated people buying cases of claret and weekends at country hotels, never raise much money. It didn't take superhuman acuity for Jonathan to sense my doubts.

'Peter's idea was called "First Editions, Second Thoughts".'

'What's that mean?'

'It means you ask authors to revisit a first edition of their most famous and valuable work, and then to write in it throughout, to annotate it with memories, subsequent reflections, anecdotes, whatever the revisiting entails by way of thinking and feeling.'

'I get it. That sounds promising, but ...'

'I know. The question is how to get it to work. We tried, wrote a few letters, but it fizzled out. We have the goodwill of writers, and many of their direct contact details, but we simply didn't know how to do it. And now we have a proper rare book dealer on the Board, we thought you might be able to follow up. Do you think it makes any sense?'

Well, it's my job as a bookseller to source and to market literary treasures; here was a chance, if it worked, to create some. At the next Board meeting, Jonathan explained the idea, and I gave an outline of how I would go about doing it: make a list of the most desirable participants, source fine copies of their most important first editions, send them to the writer to annotate. Once we had a few major writers on board, others would pile in.

To my astonishment, I got sceptical responses from the officers of the organisation, especially the Treasurer. Who would pay for these books? How much would they cost? What would happen if they failed to sell? What if they sold but lost money? I replied, a bit miffed perhaps, that of course they will sell and we could not lose money. Treasurers have big noses and can sniff out delusions. A scheme that cannot lose money? Hah! PEN is a registered charity! He had a fiduciary responsibility.

But the only cost to PEN would be in purchasing the first editions to give to those writers who couldn't provide one, and the addition of their annotations would add substantial value to the book. If I could get, say, fifty English and Commonwealth authors to agree to annotate, that would produce substantial funds for PEN. The crucial questions, then, were which authors, and how much money?

The scepticism remained. It was still a risk, wasn't it? The answer – not at all, not the teeniest bit, nothing to fear, stop with the worrying already! – didn't satisfy the sceptics, until in one meeting I threw up my hand and said, 'Fine! I will buy all of the books out of my own pocket, and I can be reimbursed after the auction.' That did it.

To begin, I drafted an explanatory letter to my chosen authors, to explain what was surely a unique, and perhaps puzzling request: 'Feel free to scribble second thoughts, marginalia or drawings throughout the work in whatever fashion moves you, thus singling out this particular first edition and making it even more desirable for a reader or collector to want to own.' When asked what this actually entailed, I stone-walled with Humpty Dumpty's wise view that a word (such as 'annotate') can mean whatever you want it to mean. It was hardly up to me to determine how an author responded to his or her own work.

I made up a preliminary list of novelists, poets and dramatists whose annotated books I thought would be of interest and value, and sent them the letter. The responses from the writers were heartening: the idea itself appealed to many of them, and the thought that they could support PEN with a few hours' work was attractive. Some writers declined our invitation, for various reasons: Salman Rushdie, a great champion of PEN as PEN had been a great champion of him, said that revisiting *Midnight's Children* in this way simply wasn't something he could do. I understood that, and the few other writers who felt similarly. John Banville said that he hates rereading his books, but generously agreed to grit his teeth and give it a go. His annotations in his 2005 Man Booker Prize-winner *The Sea*, began with the sentence: 'Nice, the opportunity to deface one of my own books.'

But not all writers found the opportunity 'nice': Tom Stoppard found the process, as he remarked to me in an email, 'a bit artificial'. I replied that, since he often talks and writes about his past work, often in some forensic detail, all he had to do was write such commentary into one of the printed plays. 'Send the book!' he replied, and his comments on *Rosencrantz and Guildenstern are Dead* were fascinating. He began by saying: 'I wanted to call the play "Exit Rosencrantz and Guildenstern", but for the bad grammar – "Exeunt R and G" I didn't like as a title, so settled for "are dead".' Next to one scene between the protagonists, he crossed out many lines and wrote: 'Overkill!'

Lord Dalmeny, chattering, fussing and extracting like a manic dentist, was now on Lot 31, Hilary Mantel's bestseller, the 2009 Man Booker-winner *Wolf Hall*, annotated on 123 pages with over 2,500 words: 'Just for the record – I made up the affair between TC + his sister-in-law. Not without reason, but because it seems to reflect the semi-incestuous knot that Henry himself got into ...'

After the gavel went down at £16,000, I could hear people whispering to each other, as they had been since the very first lots, 'Amazing prices! Wow!' perhaps thinking that, 'Well, people overpay at charity auctions. Supporting the cause, that's what matters, bit vulgar to expect a bargain as well.'

But a bargain was exactly what they were getting. It took some time for most of us to realise this. On the night of the auction I was too frantic to sit back and assess whether these books represented value for money, or even to appreciate them fully for what they were. I so admired Hilary Mantel's apparently throwaway phrase of annotation – 'just for the record' – because in a sense she was producing the copy of record. Most of the writers were. Their books, uniquely annotated and often illustrated, are important documents in the history of literature.

In the run-up to the auction, describing the forthcoming sale to sceptical rare book dealers, archivists and librarians, trying to drum up some action, I formulated and reformulated my belief and enthusiasm about this new literary mode. I found myself enunciating each word separately, as if speaking to a foreigner with limited English. It drove me crazy:

> *The best copies of the best books by the best writers!*
> *The most intellectually interesting first editions by the most*
>   *interesting authors!*
> *The most important examples of the most important books!*

In the trade in modern first editions, high prices are often assigned not to the rarest texts and finest inscribed copies, but to the presence of dust wrappers, preferably in fine condition. To compare like with unlike: the mere presence of a pristine wrapper on a first edition of *Catcher in the Rye* will fetch a price higher than that annotated *Wolf Hall*.

It's absurd. But it accounted for the fact that rare book dealers showed little interest in the FEST project, and did not come either to the pre-sale viewing or attend the auction itself. Some dealers and librarians thought the concept, and the books resulting from it, 'artificial', which is surely based on a naïve conception of where books come from. Authors don't simply sit around thinking until an idea, wholly its own, pops up: Presto! Write! No, books and articles are suggested by friends, family, other writers, they are commissioned by magazines and newspapers, and catalysed by publishers and literary agents. Not artificial, prompted.

So far as I could ascertain, only one lot (Nick Hornby's *Fever Pitch*) sold to a rare book dealer who was in the room at Sotheby's, and that was for his own collection. This blinkered-ness was embarrassing, particularly as you might suppose booksellers would wish to support the work of English PEN, but what was even more surprising was that none of the major libraries, many of whom have extensive collections of the books and manuscripts by our writers, showed any interest either. The only books – by Barnes, McEwan and Mantel – that ended up in a collecting institution were bought by a benefactor who donated them to the Morgan Library in New York.

Hold on a bit. A confession, full disclosure: one dealer bought seven books. That would be me, bidding on behalf of clients, but doing it through several friends in the audience, lest it seem inappropriate for the organiser of the auction also to be a buyer at it, which seemed uncontroversial to me, but people love striking attitudes. But if I could buy multiple books for multiple clients, why couldn't other dealers?

As Lord Dalmeny made his way playfully through Lots 32–38 (Martell, Morpurgo, Motion, Okri, Pierre, and Pullman) there was a noticeable increase of attention in the room. People who were chatting (people talk a lot during auctions, usually too loudly) quietened and consulted their catalogue, others who had left the room for a cigarette or a pee re-emerged. The BBC and other cameramen in the aisles readied their equipment and pointed their lenses at the podium.

'Lot 39!' said Dalmeny as if shouting 'BINGO'! 'JK Rowling's *Harry Potter and the Philosopher's Stone*, first edition, extensively annotated and with 22 illustrations by the author.'

He looked round while the clichés and cameras whirled. You could have heard a pin drop, this was the jewel in the crown: the one that just might transform the auction from the

great success it already was to something, well ...
stratospheric.

It had taken many months to get Rowling to agree to
participate. An approach through Scottish PEN was attempted,
but led nowhere. As the deadline for submissions approached,
I was bemoaning this apparent impasse to my friend Philip
Errington, of the Sotheby's Book Department, when he
smiled and put his hand up to quell the flow.

'Send me your email to her,' he said, 'and I should be able
to get it to her.' As luck would have it – I'd been ready to give
up – Philip was working with Rowling on a bibliography of
her works, having met her some years previously at that
Sotheby's charity auction of *Beedle the Bard*.

I wrote an email immediately, adding the concession, or
perhaps it was an incentive, that if Rowling would agree to
annotate, the proceeds would be shared between English PEN
(2/3) and Rowling's Lumos Foundation charity (1/3). The
next afternoon I had my answer from her office. YES, Joanne
would be happy to do this, but alas did not possess a first
edition, so might we please supply one?

This would be difficult, and very expensive. Only 500
copies of the first hardback edition were printed, many of
which went to libraries. Others were purchased by unwitting
lucky enthusiasts, and the books were soon resold and sold
again. The price had gone up more precipitately than the
NASDAQ during the dotcom boom. I asked the booksellers
who specialised in *Potter* if they had a copy? No luck. And
then one popped up on the Internet, in fine condition, which
it had to be because the laminated covers – it has no dust
wrapper – tend to deteriorate quickly, and look a mess.

The price was £25,000. I rang the dealer, who lived some-
where in the American Midwest. Could he offer a trade
discount? No. But it was for charity: could he offer a charity
discount? No. Could he hold it for me for a week while I
organised payment? No. Was he prepared to send it by courier
immediately, but on approval, subject to it being as described?
There was a pause, and a grudging 'Yes'. That's how rare book
sellers have to do business.

By this time even the (no longer grudging) Treasurer of
English PEN was thoroughly on board with the project,
happy to sanction the purchase. The book arrived, and was as
described. The next day I FedExed it to Rowling's office in
Edinburgh, crossed my various and sundry digits, and waited
for developments.

In a couple of weeks I got a call. The book was ready.

'Wonderful! For goodness sake don't send it by couriers ...
I'll pop up to Edinburgh tomorrow to pick it up and bring it
back to London ...'

That wasn't necessary. The next day I had a call from
Rowling's office to say that her agent would bring it to
London himself. It was better, even, than we had hoped.
Across some fifty pages were scattered comments about the
genesis of the *Harry Potter* project: 'I wrote the book ... in
snatched hours, in clattering cafés or in the dead of night. For
me, the story of how I wrote *Harry Potter and the Philosopher's
Stone* is written invisibly on every page, legible only to me.'

Legible to us were the twenty-two drawings that are scattered throughout, in a charmingly artless style, including
images of the sleeping baby Harry Potter on the Dursleys'
doorstep, an Albus Dumbledore Chocolate Frog card, an

image of the brooding Snape, Norbert the Norwegian
Ridgeback dragon, the mirror of Erised, and a man with two
faces. There is some explanation, too, of the genesis of
Quidditch, which: '... was invented in a small hotel in
Manchester after a row with my then boyfriend. I had been
pondering the things that hold a society together, cause it to
congregate and signify its particular character and I knew I
needed a sport. It infuriates men ... which is quite satisfying
given my state of mind when I invented it.'

Once we had the book safely in its padded envelope a
sustained debate began amongst us: if *Beedle the Bard* was
worth £2 million, what was this utterly extraordinary annotated *Harry Potter* going to fetch?

'Let's not get over-excited,' I said in my most over-excited
manner, clutching our treasure to my chest, 'I'm not sure the
two are comparable. It's not about the price of *Beedle the Bard*.'

When the sale catalogue was issued, the *Harry Potter*
description contained a stipulation, forbidding the buyer and
any future owner from using the book for 'any commercial
and/or marketing purposes'. This was a trifle ambiguous but
was not intended to preclude a member of the rare book
trade buying the book, and then selling it on, as long as any
new buyer agreed to the terms of the original contract.

During the Sotheby's party before the sale began, I was
several times asked about this contractual obligation by several
prospective buyers, including one chap who said he 'had come
to buy the book'. I didn't know him: could he be counted on
either to do so, or to drive the price up? There's nothing
better than a combination of a determined buyer and an
aggressive under-bidder – which was a point I made

explicitly in my remarks from the podium, welcoming people at the evening reception.

'There are two ways you can help English PEN this evening,' I said, peering out over the audience. 'Of course the first is that you buy something. Please do. But the second is that you might aggressively make sure that whoever is buying something pays a serious price. Bid it up! Because for every increment that you force the price up, you are making a contribution to English PEN. And if you find that in a fit of passion you have unintentionally produced a newcomer to your home, never mind, once you have lived with it for a time you will come to love it.'

This produced a laugh, and a result. Perhaps many results. It was impossible to tell which under-bidders were genuine potential buyers, and which were following my advice to ramp it up. Except in the case of the *Harry Potter*. Shortly before the sale began, I was discussing the *Potter* with my friend John Simpson, formerly CEO of The Mayflower Corporation, and a mighty collector of Oscar Wilde.

'What's the *Harry Potter* going to fetch?' he asked.

'Are you interested in buying it?'

'Not at all. But it's fascinating. Will it make a fortune?'

'Nobody can tell.'

'What's your guess?'

'Well, put it this way: if someone bought it for a hundred thousand pounds they'd be getting a bargain.'

'Who'll start me off?' asked Lord Dalmeny.

'I have thirty thousand pounds ... thirty-five thousand pounds ...' There were several bids in the room, and an aggressive bidder on the phone, sometimes skipping increments, going directly from £35,000 to £50,000. Someone who knew what they were doing.

After a bid of £90,000 by Pom Harrington, the leading dealer in *Harry Potter* first editions, the bidding went to £100,000 to the telephone bidder.

There was silence in the room. People kept their hands firmly at their sides, too expensive a baby to bring home. Or was it?

From the second row came a bid from John Simpson, who then took the book up to £130,000, against the phone bidder, who quickly replied by forcing the issue up to £150,000.

Harry Dalmeny looked round beseechingly. John kept his hand down.

'All done then? I'm selling at a hundred and fifty thousand pounds . . .'

The gavel went down, a round of applause swept through the room.

At my side in the front row Peter Straus nodded to me, and raised his eyebrows.

'Fuck!' I said. Not in a good way. I'd been hoping for a lot more.

I picked up my catalogue to try to concentrate on the next lots, on several of which I had bids. I bought Colm Tóbín's *The Heather Blazing* at £15,500 – sitting next to me, Colm looked distinctly pleased – and Jeanette Winterson's *Oranges Are Not the Only Fruit* together with *Why Be Happy When You Could be Normal?* at £6,500.

At the end of the auction it was announced from the podium that the proceeds were £439,200. I immediately popped over to have a word with John Simpson.

'That was a ballsy bit of bidding, what would you have done if it'd been knocked down to you?'

'No worries,' he said, 'I'd have given it to you to sell at a profit.'

Seeing us talking, Pom Harrington wandered over.

'What do you think of the price . . .?'

'I think that's what it's worth.'

'I don't!' I said.

At that very moment I was flanked by Belinda and our friend Fiammetta Rocco, of *The Economist*, both of whom grabbed one of my arms to lead me away into the night, and out to a boozy celebratory dinner at Andrew Edmund's.

'Do NOT let a journalist hear you saying "disappointing",' said Fiammetta strictly. 'Anyway, PEN has a relatively small budget, and organisations like that can founder if you give them too much money. They're not used to it, and often make bad judgements spending it.' Everyone involved, she added – the staff at PEN, the writers, Sotheby's cataloguers, support staff and Lord Dalmeny – had been supportive, professional, and exacting.

'It's a perfect amount, and it was a perfect auction!'

A few glasses of wine later I agreed, more or less.

But I still think I could have sold that Harry Potter at a profit.

13

Not So Elementary, My Dear Watson

JAMES WATSON'S NOBEL PRIZE FOR DNA DISCOVERY
SELLS FOR RECORD £3M

Nobel Prize gold medal belonging to Watson, who co-discovered DNA in Cambridge in 1953, was first put on sale by a living recipient ...

The *Telegraph*, 5 December 2014

It was a great deal, you couldn't have made it up. Not only did Dr Watson get his money for his medal, but the buyer, the oligarch Alisher Usmanov, gave the medal back to him, pronouncing that no one should need to sell such an accolade.

'It means,' Watson told me over lunch at Claridge's, in June of 2016, 'that from now on I pay for lunches.'

He'd contacted me at the suggestion of his New York literary agent, because he wished to sell the manuscript(s) for *The Double Helix* (1968), his account of the discovery of the structure of DNA in Cambridge in 1953. He was hesitant to schedule a further sale at Christie's, because at auction the highest bidder wins, and the material may well disappear from scholarly view, into some mansion or *dacha*, tent or palace. Better, surely, to find an agent to arrange a private sale, to ensure that the material can go to an appropriate home, and be available to researchers.

Formally dressed in tweed suit and tie, James Watson rose to greet me, stiffly, and shook my hand. His gaunt face was as familiar as if he'd been in the movies, perhaps as The Scarecrow in *The Wizard of Oz*, and the waiters were more than deferential to him. He seemed to appreciate that, or perhaps he demanded it. His (much younger) wife Liz sat by his side proprietorially, and for the first half-hour said little, stroking her husband's arm, a practised, anxious, listener.

'Please call me Jim,' he said. 'Everyone does.'

We negotiated our early exchanges easily enough. His reminiscences of Cambridge in the 1950s were familiar, I'd read them before.

'Of course I already had a PhD when I got there. I didn't meet many undergraduates. They were a bit provincial.'

I nodded. 'I get that. Even ten or twelve years later, when I went up to Oxford in the middle sixties, things were much the same ...'

He looked at me with a first glimmer of interest. I'd moved up a notch in his estimation. Which college was I?

'Merton. Did a BPhil and DPhil in English. Then taught for many years at the University of Warwick ...'

We paused to peruse the menu, ordered, he chose the wine.

'I'm working,' he said, 'on my second most important book. I'm convinced I won't be at my intellectual peak until I'm ninety-five ...' He was then only eighty-eight.

'I've just reread *The Double Helix*,' I said, 'with immense pleasure. It's a remarkable sort of memoir ...'

'I think of it as a novel,' he replied. 'I had to make some things up to increase their dramatic impact. The second most important sentence in it is Crick exclaiming in the pub that we had discovered the secret of life! Of course he said no such thing!'

'He has now,' I said, and got a quick appreciative smile, and moved up another notch.

I was dying to ask him, not what was the first most important book and sentence to which he was (not) referring, but which was, say, the sixth most? With anyone else, one would have received a wry smile of recognition and self-mockery; he might well have known.

I went on to inquire – the subject was the elephant in the dining room – whether, in 1953, he had any idea where his research into genetics might lead, and what implications it might have for human society?

'None at all. We were just doing the work.'

Is it wrong of me retrospectively to suppose this incurious of him? Because once you understand the structure of the human genome, surely you begin to ask, must ask, how this structure pertains to different humans? And if it, being a structure, might be altered?

In 2007, Watson visited London to give a talk to a distinguished body of scientists. Before his lecture, he was interviewed by a journalist from the *Sunday Times*, who naturally enough asked him what problems in the world he was most exercised by.

He responded that he was 'gloomy' about Africa because 'all our social policies are based on the fact that their intelligence is the same as ours – whereas all the testing says not really.'

Did he mean that black people are less intelligent than whites?

Yes, he did. By way of evidence he added that people 'who have to deal with black employees' would know that he was speaking the truth. (On the other hand, he has claimed, blacks have the compensation of having a higher sex drive.)

These pronouncements were splashed on the front page of that week's *Sunday Times*. At first Watson denied saying such things, but the reporter had a mini tape recorder, and it was on the record. Over the next weeks he stuttered, backtracked, and apologised.

'Well, of course I did,' he said over lunch. 'I was required to apologise. But I was right. The evidence is clear, just as it is that Jews are more intelligent.'

He said this with the tone and confidence of a teller of uncomfortable truths – it is not the job of the scientist to sugar-coat the results of research. He regards himself as a moral agent, fearless, willing to accept whatever the data reveals, and to say what he thinks. He is well aware of the costs of this – after the *Sunday Times* story he lost his eminent position at the Cold Spring Harbor Laboratory – but it hasn't shut him up. I suspect he rather enjoys kicking the sacred cows. He doesn't think he is more intelligent and exacting than everyone else, he knows it.

He seems curiously unaware that these attitudes are shocking, but Liz isn't, she goes into a kind of trance as he says such things, retracts, looks down at her plate, pushes her food about.

'I remember all that,' I said, neutrally. 'It may make it more difficult to sell your manuscript ... Tell me where is it kept?'

The Double Helix manuscripts – consisting of both handwritten and typed progressive versions of the book – were on deposit at Harvard, but were owned by a family trust, and could apparently be withdrawn from the library.

'I can easily recover it if I want to sell.'

Liz began to demur, thought better of it, and stroked his arm reassuringly.

'Do you have a price in mind?'

'I want twenty million dollars.'

'Tell me how you came to that figure.'

'I want to help my two sons out for the rest of their lives, and ten million won't accomplish that.' He didn't explain why not. I didn't inquire.

In such discussions with potential clients I make it a point – it is rather against my nature – to listen more than I talk. I cannot represent someone unless I know exactly what they want, and why. I nodded, and encouraged him to continue. Not that I could have stopped him.

'It is,' he said with utter confidence – the way he said everything, really – 'the second most valuable American manuscript of the twentieth century.'

'What's the most valuable then?'

'*The Great Gatsby.*'

Comparators filled my head, as I sipped my glass of Chablis. The manuscript of Kerouac's *On the Road* sold in May of

2001 for $2.43 million. And though they were not going to come on to the market, there were the manuscripts of *The Waste Land*, *The Sun Also Rises*, and *Catcher in the Rye* to consider. Not to mention a variety of possible scientific manuscripts and historical documents. I flicked through the possibilities as we ate our fish. The manuscript of Martin Luther King's 'I Have a Dream' speech?

But there was a genre-confusion going on, and it had commercial implications: *The Double Helix* was not science (that was done in the Cavendish Laboratory in Cambridge in 1953), it was hardly even the history of science (not boring enough), nor was it (my own choice) a memoir. No, it was a novel: it was sexed up to make it zip along. *The Double Helix* was not the main event, merely a (semi-fictional) account of that event published fifteen years later. Watson was clearly making a category mistake. The manuscript of his rather wonderful memoir was not a ground-breaking document, not even a fancy prize-medal-commemorating one. Could it be worth as much as Kerouac's masterpiece, written in 1951 in a drug-and-caffeine-fuelled frenzy over three weeks, on a 120ft continuous scroll of paper? I know which I would rather have.

The alarm bells were blaring, but I ignored them as blithely as if I were a first-class passenger in the dining room of the *Titanic* with, surely my dear, ample time to finish that excellent bottle of claret and to light a good cigar. (The dining room at Claridge's is a perfect setting for such smugness.)

If it was foolish of Watson to think his manuscript so valuable, was it stupid of me to countenance his appraisal, not to demur from the very onset of our relationship? The only result of my doing so, however, would have been that he'd have scoffed the last of his gâteau, wiped his chops, and headed home. It was clearly going to be impossible to dissuade him from his fantasy. The only way that might happen was slowly: start with his delusional valuation, demonstrate that the market did not support it, and descend slowly to something much more realistic. That was my strategy, and it was exceedingly unlikely to work. But a 10 per cent commission on even a few million was well worth the effort.

Watson's belief was that 'some billionaire' might buy his manuscript, and donate it to an institution. (Or perhaps give it back to him?) This is a common enough fantasy about how the mega-rich operate. Many years before I had been instructed by William Golding to find a buyer for the manuscript of *Lord of the Flies*, for 'a million', on the grounds that surely 'some rich American or Japanese' would pay that. When I consulted friends in the book trade and at the auction houses, I got no valuation of over £250,000. I told Golding that we would not be able to find a buyer at his price. He was undeterred from his assessment of his manuscript, but immediately revised his valuation of me.

'The problem, Jim, is that a sale to an American institution will be impossible ... given the sensitivities of today's undergraduates, I suspect there would be a demonstration on the steps of the Library on the very day that a University announced the acquisition of your work.'

'I blame the women,' he said, oddly.

'Why is that?'

'Genetically, women have no sense of humour.'

I made no attempt to follow this line of thought, if it could be so classified. It made no sense adducing counter-examples:

Dorothy Parker! No more than it would refute the claim about blacks to shout 'Barack Obama'! That would only prove how methodologically naïve I am.

It was no wonder to me, by this time, that the eminent biologist EO Wilson once labelled Watson 'the most unpleasant human being I have ever met'. Yet – I feel rather rueful admitting this – I was rather enjoying our lunch. There's something utterly fascinating in meeting someone not so much on, as totally off, the spectrum. (Amusingly, he once diagnosed both Crick and Rosalind Franklin as 'autistic'.)

'Tell me,' he said, perhaps seeing the clouds of doubt in my eyes, 'how many staff do you employ? Five or six?'

That would be none. I hardly employ myself a lot of the time, until I find a project that animates me. This one did.

'I use freelance people as needed: cataloguers, appraisers, marketing experts ...'

'And how do you propose to market my manuscript?'

I had a preliminary answer to this, but was reluctant to give it, and even more reluctant to carry on until I had his assurance that he had title, and the right to sell.

'I could agree to a two-year period for you to find a buyer,' he said.

'Let's hold off on our strategy for now. I will wait for you to confirm that you are able to sell the material, and that I am appointed as your agent at a commission of 10 per cent.'

Of course Christie's would have offered to represent him for free, as it were, by waiving their seller's premium. And – one could see the thought in his eyes – they'd do a hell of a lot better job of selling the manuscripts than this Gekoski person.

A few moments later lunch was over, I thanked him warmly for an unforgettable experience, and he gave me an inscribed offprint of one of his articles. I never heard from him again, though his secretary at the Cold Spring Laboratory emailed to inform me that he had 'made other plans'. Good luck, I thought. I wouldn't have had the faintest chance of success.

Neither did he, so far as I can tell. He'd returned to Christie's, convinced that they could market his manuscript more efficiently than an independent, un-staffed dealer in England: the great auction houses are excellent at hyping up material, blowing trombones and distributing glossy brochures, and marketing internationally. The only problem was that Christie's weren't buying Watson's fantastical asking price. Not for a second, not even close, not even close to close. I rather admired them for this. Since which time I have scanned their auction catalogues for an entry regarding the manu-script, but none has appeared. It may be that the process was halted when he had a serious car accident, driving into a 20ft ditch in 2018. (He'd also had a car crash in 1984, and I'll bet he ranks them in order of seriousness.)

Curiously, *The Double Helix* was soon to reappear on my biblio-radar, coming from quite a different direction. Within a year of my lunch with Watson at Claridge's, I was involved in the sale of the archive of Weidenfeld & Nicolson Publishers. The Weidenfeld files had long been stored, along with the archives of Victor Gollancz and JM Dent, in that immense warehouse in Littlehampton, and no one had consulted or arranged them for many decades.

Weidenfeld was a good literary and historical publishing house, which had produced books by Cecil Beaton, Saul

Bellow, Cyril Connolly, Margaret Drabble, Martin Gilbert, Claude Lévi-Strauss, Mary McCarthy, Norman Mailer, Vladimir Nabokov, Edna O'Brien, and Harold Wilson. The editorial files for all of their books were complete, save for those relating to *Lolita* (1959), which I presume had been taken away by George Weidenfeld for safe-keeping. The rest of the material was fascinating, but – surely! – none of it was as important, or as valuable, as the files for *The Double Helix*.

If one could only find them, which took several long, irritating and dusty days. The filing cabinets were distributed almost randomly round the immense room, and while the individual files were orderly, they were not alphabetised by author in the cabinets. Papers were squashed in and overflowing, and I could never tell what I might find next. This may sound like treasure-hunty fun, but it wasn't, particularly in mid-winter, wearing an overcoat, scarf and sometimes even fingerless gloves.

On the afternoon that I finally located the three *Double Helix* files, I laid them out excitedly, and started reading and counting. Eighteen letters from Watson, and many more from various lawyers, editors, and the publishers, as well as many from luminaries asked to give a puff for the new book. A surprising number, Isaiah Berlin amongst them, declined, some because they didn't much admire Watson's relaxed form of narration.

The final drafts of the book met with strenuous objections from Watson's colleagues: his partner Francis Crick, and fellow DNA researcher Maurice Wilkins. There was also the likelihood that Watson's account would offend the family of the late X-ray crystallographer Rosalind Franklin, whose photographs of the double helix structure preceded, and to a degree initiated, Watson and Crick's 'discovery'. Watson pushed her right out of the story, but not before commenting on how badly she dressed. He was later to call her 'a loser'. (This later became a favoured phrase of Donald Trump, a man whom Watson admired for his capacity to 'control the narrative', though he thought him a buffoon.)

Though the book was initially intended for American publication by the Harvard University Press, the libel threats were apparently so bothersome that the university eventually declined to publish, allowing former HUP director Tom Wilson to negotiate to transfer the rights when he joined the new commercial publisher Athenaeum. Weidenfeld & Nicolson had been offered the British rights early on by HUP, and they remained steadfast in their commitment to the text throughout the protracted libel negotiation process, during which both Crick and Wilkins threatened lawsuits.

Once he'd read the submitted manuscript, Crick's responses to the English publisher were scathing: a letter dated 13 April 1967, objected strongly and in great detail to the contents and tone of the book, then titled *Honest Jim*. Crick maintained that Watson's account was not a history of the scientific discovery, as stated in the preface, but a self-aggrandising form of autobiography: 'Should you persist in regarding your book as history I should add that it shows such a naive and egotistical view of the subject as to be scarcely credible ...' Even considered as autobiography, Crick maintained, the book is: '... misleading and in bad taste ... and the portrait painted of me is a caricature, and could well injure me professionally ... Nor can there be any reasonable doubt that the book, not being a serious historical work, is an unnecessary invasion of my privacy.'

Watson's account of their work together, Crick concluded, was as simplified and vulgar as 'the lower class of women's magazines . . . the history of scientific discovery is displayed in the manuscript as gossip.' (This sounds damagingly superior, until one recalls Robert Oppenheimer's observation that today 'the most advanced science takes the form of international gossip'.)

In addition to the libel issue, there was sustained debate concerning the book's title. Watson initially wanted to call it *Honest Jim*, an amusing but probably unwitting conflation of the common description of President Lincoln (Honest Abe) with the title of Kingsley Amis's novel about the follies of academic life (*Lucky Jim*). Watson then suggested the title *Base Pairs* – which I like to think of as a reference to himself and Crick – and then *The Golden Helix*, before settling, reluctantly, on the simple and classic title which the book now bears.

With Watson's confidence in his own financial value still ringing in my ears, I decided that the Watson files were worth more than the rest of the Weidenfeld & Nicolson archival files combined. The figure of £100,000 popped into my head, and refused to budge. Why not? The discovery of the nature of DNA was arguably the great scientific breakthrough of the twentieth century! And here were the inward workings, the debates, the big egos and bruised egos: the real nitty gritty. At least £100,000!

And this, of course, caused a new problem. The archive should be kept intact. But if it were, the Watson files would not glow with the same intensity as they would if extracted and marketed separately. If the manuscript of *The Double Helix* was worth (could one surmise?) something in the low millions, then this associated material must be of very considerable value. Christie's would surely jump at the chance. And, of course, there was a possible buyer in Watson himself, who might wish to acquire the letters to protect the value of his original manuscript, perhaps even to enhance it,

As a dealer I often don't know what to do, or quite how to do it. First, of course, I needed to catalogue and to describe the *Double Helix* files, or better yet get my associate Laura Massey, herself a dealer in scientific material, to do it for me. And then, unsure what to do next, I got on the phone to make the appropriate inquiries. How important were these files? How much might they be worth?

As I had with the manuscript of *Lord of the Flies*, I took some soundings, none of which supported my initial optimistic appraisal. After all (as if I needed to be reminded) *The Double Helix* is 'only' a memoir, and of the many Watson letters in the Weidenfeld & Nicolson files, only three or four had significant content. I was almost relieved to accept this advice, and to return the files to their rightful place in the archive, where they may now be consulted in their new home at The Firestone Library at Princeton.

I'd spent a considerable amount of time, thought and energy on Dr Watson's *Double Helix*. I might have earned $2 million if I had improbably sold it at the original asking price, perhaps to Alisher Usmanov, who might have been re-enlisted, or Microsoft's Paul Allen, who had invited Honest Jim to his yacht cruise honouring the people who had most influenced him, or to the wayward Elon Musk, who is as keen as Crick on the secret of life. Or perhaps to Mr Bezos, who once improbably paid £2 million for *Beedle the Bard*?

As it is, I have nothing to show for my efforts save this story. I call that a satisfactory deal, I couldn't have made it up.

Afterword

Booksellers, if sometimes retiring, rarely retire. For many of us it is a vocation, rather than a job, which can be practised to the very edges of senility, and sometimes beyond. You can still hunt treasure even when you don't remember where it is. But if we carry on, it is not always a comfortable process, and I am unabashedly aware that this book is occasionally nostalgic and grumpy, as well as celebratory. If you've practised any trade for well on fifty years, it is too easy, and in a way too agreeable, to compare the past favourably with the present. The good old days!

Things have changed. Even the staid auction houses have online sales these days, and it will not be long before there are no live book auctions to attend. And that is worse than sad, not merely because it can be quite fun buying, or more often failing to buy, in the auction rooms, but because unless you can examine a book physically it is impossible accurately to gauge its condition. You value books with your eyes and fingers. (The better auction houses still have their books on pre-sale display for viewing, but this only serves local buyers.) Rare book dealers sell books on approval: if not as described, indeed if you just don't like the look of it, you send a book back, no questions asked. I am told by several major auctioneers that this will soon be the case with books purchased online at auction.

When I began collecting books, and in my early days in the trade, private collectors rarely purchased directly at auction, preferring to nominate a dealer to do so on their behalf. One of the great post-war dealers, Margie Cohen, of House of Books in New York, once shooed away one of her young collectors when he had the temerity to attend a live auction.

'Go away!' she said. 'This is where I work!'

He stayed, and bid aggressively on a couple of books he wanted badly. In each case Margie stared at him venomously, and outbid him. The next morning she rang him to offer him the books at a margin of 10 per cent, on the condition that he 'never does that again!' He bought the books, and never did.

You'd never get away with that these days. Though the majority of books at auction are purchased by members of the book trade, private collectors are now ubiquitous in the auction rooms, cutting out the middle man. I charge 10 per cent to represent a client at auction, and I'm worth it. I can assess the quality of books expertly, know how the systems work, what the reserves are, who the competition will be and how to come to some pre-sale understanding of what the market looks like. I also know more about the individual books than the great majority of my customers. But increasingly I see them sitting there in the rooms, filling their boots, and emptying mine.

It was once the case that the most serious and richest collectors had a favourite dealer, sometimes a couple of dealers, who took responsibility for growing and curating their collection. Two of the greatest experiences of my dealing life have been acting as sole buyer for the magnificent collections of Stanley Seeger (who collected Conrad) and John Simpson (who collected Wilde). I like to think that their holdings had a depth and quality that had something of my imprimatur on them. And when their books eventually ended up at Sotheby's – alas! – I could have given good advice to several of the major private buyers who attended the sale. But they never asked, and bought widely and (in my view) not entirely wisely. These days every person is his own teacher, lawyer, doctor. We're all in the know! Google it! Who needs to see a specialist when you can consult thousands of them? If you only knew which were trustworthy.

I regret the gradual decline of connoisseurship, a term more often associated with the art market, but which can be pertinent to sophisticated book collecting. My customer and friend the New York gallerist Sean Kelly, spent twenty years building an extensive James Joyce collection, that he recently donated to the Morgan Library. Sean brought the same stringent discrimination to book collecting that he did to his work in his art gallery: 'I want to do my homework, have the best possible information available and find the best possible example of the piece I am looking for and then be able to contextualise it qualitatively, historically and aesthetically to make the most informed evaluation/decision about the work ... Of course taste plays a part in it, but being dependent on scholarship really should elevate it above a consideration in which taste is a significant factor.'

That sets a high standard, and one finds it only infrequently.

★

You may be hoping, as this book closes, for some advice about collecting: how to go about it, and whom to collect. Yet it is surely clear by now that my wisdom, such as it is, only operates intermittently, and that I am an unreliable guide to, well, most anything. I warned you about this at the start. A passion for books, like passions in love, can lead in unexpected directions. I have a friend who is an omnivorous collector, who for many years bought the first novel of every writer published in England, on the grounds that this would certainly locate the coming stars in both literary and financial terms. Which it did: a few novels jumped off the shelves, worth hundreds of pounds rather than the original tenner. There were also thousands of books worth nothing.

Was that foolish of him? I thought so then, but that was foolish of me. Good collectors should follow their instincts, and being risk-averse is a liability. One of my most active American customers, who has a gigantic collection of first editions, once said to me that 'I never make a mistake', to which the reply – 'In that case you will have a big collection but never a great one ...' – would have been rude, if accurate.

Having reflected on my forty-odd years as a dealer, it appears that the most active and profitable times were in the late '80s and '90s, when treasures were still available, there were more active customers, and less competition from other English dealers. It was the end of the hegemony of Bertram Rota and George Sims, but preceded the coming of Peter Harrington and Christiaan Jonkers: a fortunate time for me to begin. I had, then, the benefit of the acuity of Peter Selley, who as we were riding this commercial wave, came into the office one morning looking worried, took off his coat, made coffee, and invited me to sit down.

'I'm worried about the business,' he said.

That was surprising. Our last few catalogues had done very well.

'Tell me why.'

'We haven't made a bad mistake in six months.'

A wonderful encapsulation of a necessary truth: if you are going to find and buy the best things, you often have to work quickly, make an immediate decision at a book fair or when making a phone call to order from a catalogue. And in buying thus aggressively, sometimes you will have misjudged the importance of a book or manuscript, or valued it incorrectly. Though the mere fact that an item does not sell, often for years, does not mean you have mispriced it. It just hasn't met its proper owner yet. You have to be patient. But I'm not. I hate books that sit on the shelves for years, enhancing my 'inventory', and will usually sell them off at a modest profit or even a loss, just to keep the money moving about. From the point of view of a small dealer, cash flow is as important as profitability.

Peter's perception worked for us as dealers, so too should it work for collectors. (Yes, I began by promising not to give advice, but I didn't mean it.) Don't be afraid to make a mistake. I have had numerous discussions over many years with collectors who would shrug their shoulders, and laugh at the foolish things they bought when they were starting out.

'Think of it as your college education,' I'd say, 'it's how you learn. And the more you learn, the better your decisions will be, and you'll buy better books . . .'

My collector friends would nod, semi-attentively, knowing that more was coming.

'... And the other thing you need to do is to keep learning!' By which I meant, from ... er, a good dealer. Stories and examples would flow: garrulousness is the final symptom and indulgence of our trade.

One customer, hearing I was writing a memoir of my adventures, nodded sagely. 'I see,' he said: 'GEKOSKI: from modest beginning to immodest end!'

I was shocked by this *mot*.

'End!' I remonstrated. 'Book dealers don't have ends, they have deaths, the only retirement we will tolerate. Until the day, well, we go on and on, and on.'

Acknowledgements

My first thanks are due to my friend and literary agent Peter Straus, himself a passionate and immensely knowledgeable book collector, to whom this book is most appropriately and gratefully dedicated.

Various readers have helped me to avoid those infelicities, errors and oversights to which I am increasingly prone. I am most grateful for the unrelentingly accurate perception of my wife Belinda and sister Ruthie, and to various friends associated with the rare book trade who cast their forensic eyes on earlier versions of the text: Steve Enniss, Philip Errington, Jonathan Fishburn, Warwick Gould, Declan Kiely, Peter Selley, and James Stourton.

Various bits of the John Fowles, Victor Gollancz and 'Stop! Thief!' chapters are adapted from my *Guardian* 'Finger on the Page' column.

I am so fortunate to be published by Constable, where the standards of editing and design are so agreeable and exacting: to Andreas Campomar, for his continued encouragement, input, and support, and to Claire Chesser, Jon Davies